The Development of Western Civilization

*Narrative Essays in the History of Our Tradition from
Its Origins in Ancient Israel and Greece to the Present*

Edited by Edward W. Fox
Professor of Modern European History
Cornell University

ANCIENT ISRAEL

By HARRY M. ORLINSKY

Ancient Israel

HARRY M. ORLINSKY

Hebrew Union College—Jewish Institute of Religion
New York

*

SECOND EDITION

Cornell University Press

ITHACA AND LONDON

First published 1960 by Cornell University Press
First printing, Cornell Paperbacks, 1960

First edition 1954
Second edition 1960

International Standard Book Number 0-8014-9849-x
Printed in the United States of America by Vail-Ballou Press, Inc.

Cornell University Press strives to use environmentally responsible suppliers and materials to the fullest extent possible in the publishing of its books. Such materials include vegetable-based, low-VOC inks and acid-free papers that are recycled, totally chlorine-free, or partly composed of nonwood fibers. Books that bear the logo of the FSC (Forest Stewardship Council) use paper taken from forests that have been inspected and certified as meeting the highest standards for environmental and social responsibility. For further information, visit our website at www.cornellpress.cornell.edu.

20 22 24 26 28 30   Paperback printing   29 27 25 23 21 19

Foreword

THE proposition that each generation must rewrite history is more widely quoted than practiced. In the field of college texts on western civilization, the conventional accounts have been revised, and sources and supplementary materials have been developed; but it is too long a time since the basic narrative has been rewritten to meet the rapidly changing needs of new college generations. In the mid-twentieth century such an account must be brief, well written, and based on unquestioned scholarship and must assume almost no previous historical knowledge on the part of the reader. It must provide a coherent analysis of the development of western civilization and its basic values. It must, in short, constitute a systematic introduction to the collective memory of that tradition which we are being asked to defend. This series of narrative essays has been undertaken in an effort to provide such a text for the introductory history survey course offered in the College of Arts and Sciences of Cornell University. It is being published in the present form in the belief that the requirements of this one course reflect a need that is coming to be widely recognized.

Now that the classic languages, the Bible, the great historical novels, even most non-American history, have dropped out of the normal college preparatory program, it is imperative that a text in the history of European civilization be fully self-explanatory. This means not only that it must begin at the beginning, with the origins of our civilization in ancient Israel and Greece, but that it must introduce every name or event that takes an integral place in the account and ruthlessly delete all others no matter how firmly imbedded in historical protocol. Only thus simplified and complete will the narrative present a sufficiently clear outline of those major trends and developments that have led from the beginning of our recorded time to the most pressing of our current problems. This simplification, however, need not involve intellectual dilution or evasion. On the contrary, it can effectively raise rather than lower the level of presentation. It is on this assumption that the present series has been based, and each contributor has been urged to write for a mature and literate audience. It is hoped, therefore, that the essays may also prove profitable and rewarding to readers outside the college classroom.

The plan of the first part of the series was to sketch, in related essays, the narrative of our history from its origins to the eve of the French Revolution; each was written by a recognized scholar and was designed to serve as the basic reading for one week in a semester course. The developments of the nineteenth and twentieth centuries will be covered in a succeeding series which will provide the same quantity of reading material for each week of the second semester. This scale of presentation has been adopted in the conviction that any understanding of the central problem of the preservation of the integrity and dignity of the individual human being depends first on an examination of the origins of our tradition in the politics and philosophy of the ancient Greeks and the religion of the ancient

Hebrews and then on a relatively more detailed knowledge of its recent development within our industrial urban society.

The decision to devote equal space to twenty-five centuries and to a century and a half was based on analogy with the human memory. Those events most remote tend to be remembered in least detail but often with a sense of clarity and perspective that is absent in more recent and more crowded recollections. If the roots of our tradition must be identified, their relation to the present must be carefully developed. The nearer the narrative approaches contemporary times, the more difficult and complicated this becomes. Recent experience must be worked over more carefully and in more detail if it is to contribute effectively to an understanding of the contemporary world.

It may be objected that the series attempts too much. The attempt is being made, however, on the assumption that any historical development should be susceptible of meaningful treatment on any scale and in the realization that a very large proportion of today's college students do not have more time to invest in this part of their education. The practical alternative appears to lie between some attempt to create a new brief account of the history of our tradition and the abandonment of any serious effort to communicate the essence of that tradition to all but a handful of our students. It is the conviction of everyone contributing to this series that the second alternative must not be accepted by default.

In a series covering such a vast sweep of time, few scholars would find themselves thoroughly at home in the fields covered by more than one or two of the essays. This means, in practice, that almost every essay should be written by a different author. In spite of apparent drawbacks, this procedure promises real advantages. Each contributor will be in a position to set higher standards of accuracy and insight in an essay encompassing a major portion of the field of his life's work than could ordinarily be expected in surveys of some ten or twenty centuries. The inevitable discontinuity of style and interpretation could be modified by editorial co-ordination; but it was felt that some discontinuity was in itself desirable. No illusion is more easily acquired by the student in an elementary course, or is more prejudicial to the efficacy of such a course, than that a single smoothly articulated text represents the very substance of history itself. If the shift from author to author, week by week, raises difficulties for the beginning student, they are difficulties that will not so much impede his progress as contribute to his growth.

This essay, *Ancient Israel*, by Mr. Harry M. Orlinsky, is written to provide a brief narrative account of the history of the peoples who created the Hebrew Bible and, at the same time, to outline the integral relationship between the development of their society and the growth of the Biblical tradition. The importance of this subject can hardly be overstated. Not only do we draw our earliest and deepest social and moral—not to mention religious—concepts from the experiences of ancient Israel, but throughout its entire history western European civilization has maintained the Bible as the central document of its cultural inheritance. Therefore, any heir of the western European tradition who would understand the development of his society must at once look for its earliest roots in Biblical society and study not only the content, but the expression, of its principal moral precepts in the Biblical writings. It is hoped that this essay will provide an introduction to both aspects of the subject and, while indicating the significance of the historical origins of our tradition, will lead the reader to return to a new reading and new understanding of the Bible itself. All English translations of the Hebrew text of the Bible cited in this essay are the author's own; he consulted occasionally the Jewish Publication Society translation (Philadelphia, 1917) and the Revised Standard Version (New York, 1952). Chapter and verse numbers refer both to the Hebrew Bible and to the King James Version and the Revised Standard Version unless otherwise indicated.

Any study of the Bible encounters serious obstacles. Not only do religious convictions and emotions make any clear summary extremely difficult, but in recent years the complexity of the subject has been vastly increased by startling archaeological discoveries in Israel and the Near East. So far this wealth of new materials has not been fully assimilated. Needless to say, the organization of such a range of new materials within such a complex field has called for frequent consultation with other scholars. Both author and editor wish to express their gratitude to Dr. Solomon Grayzel, Dr. Benjamin Maisler (Mazar), Dr. Ellis Rivkin, Dr. G. Ernest Wright, and Dr. Kenneth E. Stein. Miss Linda Altman, with the aid of Dr. Israel Renov, is responsible for the maps. Mr. Sanford Elwitt assisted in the preparation of this revised edition.

EDWARD WHITING FOX

Ithaca, New York
March, 1960

Contents

Maps

Introduction

THE tribes of Israel, though small in numbers and relatively late to arrive, were destined to remain unique among the many peoples who appeared in western Asia at the dawn of history. Out of their way of life grew three great religions, the Jewish, the Christian, and the Moslem.

The history and religious experiences of the Israelites are interwoven in a collection of writings called the Bible. No other single book, or collection of books, has played so important and prolonged a role in the development of western civilization. Indeed, the simple use of the word Bible, which derives from Greek *ta biblia* "the books," with no more identification than the capital "B," points to its significance as "the Book" par excellence.

Influence of the Bible

No other description is needed because the Bible has constituted the supreme religious and moral fount and authority for the numerous nations who have professed the Hebrew, Christian, and Moslem faiths. The moral codes of western Europe have drawn heavily on the ethical teachings of the Bible, particularly on the concepts of social justice which the prophets so forthrightly and dramatically expressed. Indeed, it is generally accepted that the spirit and the democratic ideals of the Constitution of the United States derive in some measure from this Biblical inheritance.

As literature, too, and as a factor in the development of the literature of western culture, the Bible has no equal. There is scarcely a book in the Bible which has not been described at some time as a literary masterpiece. The Book of Job was called by Carlyle "the grandest book ever written with pen." The Book of Ruth has frequently been cited as a model of short-story writing. Such books as Psalms and the Song of Songs have probably never been matched. If, as has been said, great literature is the expression of arresting thoughts in brilliant diction, then the poetry of Amos, Isaiah, Jeremiah, and other prophets are supreme examples of their kind.

In the matter of influence, it is generally recognized that English literature cannot be understood apart from the Bible. In its classical English form, the King James Version, the Bible has constituted from the beginning a standard of prose style. No other single work, be it Latin, Greek, or English, has so deeply affected the style and thinking of English writers.

What Is the Bible?

The Bible is a collection of various kinds of writings composed in different periods which came in time to be regarded as divinely inspired sacred scripture. These writings deal with the career of Israel from its beginning shortly after the twentieth century B.C. until the successful Maccabean war of independence of the Jews against hellenistic Syria in 165 B.C. To the Jews, the Bible consists of twenty-four books. During the first four centuries A.D. the Christian

Church compiled an additional twenty-seven books, and named them the New Testament, to distinguish them from the Old Testament, the term which it came to use for the Hebrew Bible. In addition, the Roman Catholic Church recognized several other books, which it introduced into the Old Testament. The Protestant Church, however, followed the Jewish tradition in rejecting these additional books, which are now generally known as the Apocrypha. For the purposes of this essay the Bible will be accepted to mean the twenty-four books of the Hebrew Bible.

The first, and most authoritative, division of the Hebrew Bible is the Law, or the Five Books of Moses, sometimes called the Pentateuch or Torah. These five books include Genesis, Exodus, Leviticus, Numbers, and Deuteronomy. This section contains two kinds of material: historical and legal, both terms being taken in their widest sense. The historical data relate the story of mankind, as understood by the Biblical writers, from the Creation until the days of Abraham (Genesis 1–11), proceeding from there to the career of the Hebrews in Canaan, Egypt, and the wilderness of Sinai, up to the death of Moses on the eve of the invasion of Canaan in the thirteenth century B.C. The legal part details the civil as well as the religious constitution of Israel.

The second great division of the Bible, the Prophets, consists of eight books and covers a period lasting about 750 years. In this epoch, Canaan was conquered, Israel's united and divided kingdoms rose and fell, and the state of Judah and the Temple of Solomon were restored, in part, after the Babylonian Exile, at the end of the sixth century B.C.

During this phase, the role of the prophetic movement was dominant. First of all, its adherents took the royal archives and other source material and wove them together carefully and vividly into a social and political history of Israel, carving out for themselves, in the process, a reputation as the world's first systematic historians. The books of Joshua, Judges, I and II Samuel, and I and II Kings—these books are sometimes called the Former Prophets—constitute this great achievement. Secondly, in intervening in the political and social life of their fellow Israelites, the prophets expressed their ideas so forthrightly and in such beautiful and powerful poetry that they placed themselves forever among the greatest social moralists of all time. The books of Isaiah, Jeremiah, Ezekiel (the so-called Major Prophets) and the twelve so-called Minor Prophets—among whom Hosea, Amos, and Micah stand out—are the repository of this unsurpassed material.

The third and final division of the Bible is called the Writings, or the Hagiographa. This section consists of eleven books which run a considerable gamut in variety of style and content, and nearly every one of which is a classic in its own right. Devotional literature is well represented by the familiar Book of Psalms. Wisdom literature, the speculation of what constitutes the good life and the practical means of achieving it, is exhibited in such books as Proverbs, Job, and Ecclesiastes. The Song of Songs is a lyrical poem of love, tender and passionate; in later times the lover and his beloved became identified with God and His beloved people Israel. The Book of Daniel, in its final form a product of the second century B.C., tells a dramatic story of the purported career of a Judean youth living in the Babylonian Exile in the days of Nebuchadnezzar (early six century B.C.), a time which to this day symbolizes for the Jews the pit of despair. Daniel's dreams and visions, which among other things supposedly foretell Maccabean victory over Syria about 165 B.C., became the forerunner and model of the apocalypses or supernatural revelations which appeared first in Jewish and then in Christian literature. The memoirs of Ezra and Nehemiah constitute both interesting autobiography and important source material for the restoration of Judea after the Babylonian Exile. These postexilic memoirs appear to have been edited by the person who wrote the Book of Chronicles, which provide a survey of Biblical history from Adam to Nehemiah (about 400 B.C.). Chronicles is the last of the twenty-four books of the Hebrew Bible.

The Bible as History: The Role of Archaeology

The Bible is the major source for our knowledge of the history of Israel in ancient times; yet its value for the historian has not always been appreciated sufficiently.

Until the eighteenth century the Bible was generally accepted as a trustworthy history of antiquity. The Book, indeed, was regarded as being literally true, the Creation, the Flood, Noah's Ark, the walls of Jericho, and all. But as the Age of Reason dawned and in turn gave way to nineteenth-century philosophies of evolution and scientific materialism, the Bible, in common with the New Testament and all records of antiquity, Greek, Roman, and the rest, came to be very considerably discounted as a reliable basis for the reconstruction of history.

The heroic doings of the patriarchs, Abraham, Isaac, and Jacob, as described in the Book of Genesis, were discounted as mere myth. The very existence of Moses was doubted. Joshua was believed to have had little or nothing to do with the Israelite conquest of Canaan. David and Solomon were considered greatly overrated. The story of the Babylonian Exile was relegated to the realm of fiction. And so on.

With the more recent archaeological discoveries and analysis of the ancient Near East today, however, the pendulum has now swung considerably the other way. Modern historians do not, to be sure, accept every part of the Bible equally as literal fact. Yet they have come to accept much of the Biblical data as constituting unusually reliable historical documents of antiquity, documents which take on new meaning and pertinence when they are analyzed in the light of the newly discovered extra-Biblical sources. The civilizations which flourished in the Fertile Crescent of old are better known today than anyone before World War I thought possible. The ancient Near East can now be seen from a thoroughly new perspective, and so it has become necessary to re-examine the Biblical record in the light of our broadened understanding.

The Bible as Sacred History and Its Interpretation

The major problems that confront the modern historian in handling the Bible as a source are twofold. First, he cannot fulfill his task when his materials are inadequate and of uncertain authorship and date. Only occasionally can a Biblical book, or its component parts, be ascribed to a definite time, place, author, and purpose; and, furthermore, extensive as the extra-Biblical material has become, it generally suffices only for the most general sort of corroboration or criticism of the texts. Secondly, in the handling of the Biblical material there is the major problem of discovering the fundamental economic, social, and political background from documents couched almost exclusively in religious terminology.

Those who were responsible for the composition of the Hebrew Bible believed that what they uttered and wrote derived from the God who had entered into a mutual Covenant with Israel. According to the terms of the Covenant, God loved and protected Israel and no other people, and Israel worshiped no other god but Him. The modern historian, however, cannot accept such an interpretation, but must seek—behind the religious terminology—the same kind of documented human story, with an examination of its underlying dynamics, that would be his proper objective in any other field. Otherwise he would achieve no more than a compilation of myths, chronicles, annals, oracles, autobiographies, court histories, personal apologia.

The historian cannot regard any human activity or statement, be it religious or secular, sacred or profane, as beyond his domain. His competence is limited only by the nature and adequacy of his sources. The limitations inherent in the Biblical sources thus militate against an historical reconstruction which will be clear in every respect; in spite of these inherent difficulties, scholarly researches have been supplying flashes of light where none existed before. So the work of interpretation goes on, some results of which form the basis of this essay.

CHAPTER I

The Fertile Crescent:
Hebrew Origins

THE Near East, that quadrangle of land lying between the Mediterranean, the Caspian and Red Seas, and the Persian Gulf, and connecting Asia with Africa, is in general a barren and uninviting area. Running across it, however, from the alluvial flatlands of the Tigris and Euphrates in the southeast through Syria in the northwest, and then curving down along the coast of Palestine to the Nile Delta, lies a crescent-shaped region of rich, well-watered land (see Map I). It was in this Fertile Crescent that the first great civilizations appeared and that man first made the transition from hunting, fishing, and cave dwelling to systematic farming within an organized community. From this focus, the new mode of civilization extended to lower Mesopotamia, and from there to the Syro-Palestinian coast, to Egypt, to the Anatolian plateau, to the Indus Valley in Pakistan, to Crete, and to Greece.

The Ancient Near East

This change began during the latter stages of the Neolithic or Late Stone Age, about 5500–4000 B.C. In ever-

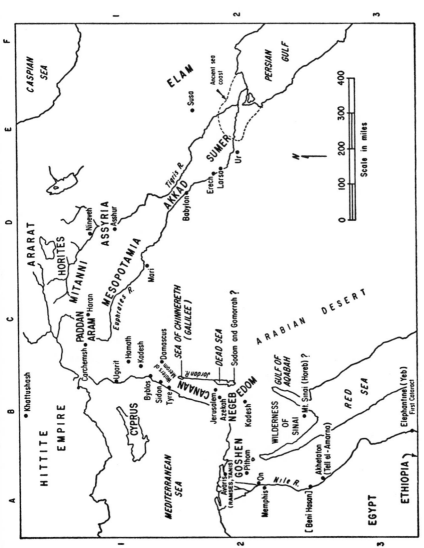

I. The ancient Near East in the patriarchal period (second millennium B.C.).

increasing numbers people learned to cultivate cereal grasses and prepare more grain than was immediately needed. Once there were food surpluses, latent human energies were released. The art of animal husbandry, of making wattle huts from mud smeared on sticks—these and other advances occurred in this period. The first crude villages appeared, sometimes, as at Jericho, in association with a shrine.

A series of metallurgical discoveries accelerated this process of social organization. During the Chalcolithic, or Copper-Stone Age, about 4000–3300 B.C., man learned how to smelt copper for use in tools, weapons, and ornaments, and gradually this malleable, if none-too-plentiful, substance superseded stone. Silver and lead came into use in several parts of the Near East, and tin (in bronze) had been discovered, though it was only rarely used, before 3000 B.C. Other technical advances followed. The wheel and the plough were invented, and a rudimentary division of labor was introduced. Houses made of mud brick replaced mud-walled huts, and in the manufacture of the bricks themselves fine-stone aggregate eventually replaced chopped straw. Houses came to have wooden roofs and even smoothly plastered walls sometimes decorated with geometric patterns in several colors.

During the Early Bronze Age, about 3300–2000 B.C., Sumer, Akkad, Egypt, and other dynastic civilizations emerged. Villages grew into cities, canals were dug to irrigate the land, men labored in organized groups. The early Egyptian dynasts built pyramid tombs, and the rulers of Mesopotamia erected structures in the form of tiered brick mounds, the ziggurats. Pictographic and cuneiform writing were invented, enabling the priestly and ruling classes to keep records and other professional data, such as magical formulae. Henceforth, too, knowledge could be stored for the use of posterity.

Growth of Cities

By this time man had become in every sense a thinking, planning, and articulate human being, with a clear idea of hierarchy in respect of class and occupation. As we have noted, villages which once had consisted of patriarchal family groups coalesced into cities, and these cities merged into "city-states," that is, urban centers controlling satellite territory. The family commune was replaced by a governing assembly of adult freemen, usually headed by a council of elders. Women, children, slaves, and the unpropertied were excluded from the assemblies. Slavery had become an economic institution, the first known instance of human chattels. These early slaves were foreign captives of war.

As the population increased, the elders began to assume the right, particularly in times of crisis, of electing a king, while retaining at all times the legal right to depose him. But with still further increase in the size and complexity of human settlements, kings became a permanent feature of the prevailing social order. The idea of a dynasty, or kingly line, followed in due course. Fixed rules for adjudicating anarchic private differences appeared, and legal codes began to be compiled, of which three dating from about 2000 B.C., from about two to three centuries before the great code of Hammurabi (or Hammurapi), have now been excavated.

Mythology, Religion, and Science

When not warring, building, tilling the soil, and tending his flocks, man began to inquire about the nature of the universe and his place in it. Literary masterpieces were created in Sumerian, Akkadian (the cuneiform Semitic language of the Babylonians and Assyrians), and Egyptian. They represented an effort to determine the origin and to evaluate the activity of the sun, the moon, the planets, the other heavenly bodies; of the rain, wind, storm, and similar phenomena; of farming and shepherding; of human life and death, of the relationships among men, of the career of man on earth and thereafter; of justice, of good and evil, of reward and punishment. In brief, as today, so then too, man attempted to learn who really ruled the universe, and how to get the most out of it for himself during his relatively brief stay in this world.

In this early period, belief in the existence of the gods in the upper and nether worlds and their intervention in human affairs on earth played a dominant role in the thinking of the people. They knew little or nothing of the why and how of natural phenomena. The all-important cycle of the growth, death, and rebirth of vegetation upon which their agricultural economy depended was attributed to supernatural powers of different gradations, to higher gods and lower gods. Men explained the origin of the gods and of their functions to the best of their rather meager knowledge in the light of their geographical environment and social experience.

Mythology and religion came to be important factors in the personal and social life of men, and myths, like religions, were seized upon by those in power, as well as by those who sought to attain power, in their own interests. Kings, priests, government and military officials, landowners, merchants— all strove to make the religious and mythological thinking of the people serve their own ends. Eventually, a self-perpetuating priestly class took shape, an intelligentsia which devoted all its time to exploring and exploiting divinity.

Pantheons of gods, with appropriate mythologies and rituals of appeasement and propitiation, crystallized out of the primitive animism of prehistory, or that kind of subreligion in which all natural forces and objects are indiscriminately endowed with demonic power. Deity, like humanity, became organized.

An agricultural society needed a way of measuring time, in order to prepare for flood, drought, heat, cold, and other seasonal fluctuations. The obvious clock was the sun, moon, and the conspicuous stars, which never vary, as shepherds since time immemorial must have observed during the watches of the night. The empirical data derived from the observation of the heavenly bodies were utilized for omens. Star watching as a regular occupation naturally fell to the priests, the superior ones who could read, write, and use numbers. Thus astronomy was incorporated into the religious apparatus, and acquired ceremonial significance, both in Egypt and Mesopotamia. A knowledge of time measurement also sharpened the chronological, or historical, sense.

Hebrew Beginnings: Habiru

The Fertile Crescent, producing as it did unprecedented wealth, frequently attracted the more primitive peoples living in the grasslands and in the highlands. The archaeological work accomplished recently in this area has produced a generally clear picture of the situation. The first identifiable people to settle permanently in Mesopotamia were the Sumerians, about 3000 B.C. In the earlier part of the third millennium, many Sumerian city-states were overrun by groups of Semites, and about 2300 B.C. the first empire in history was established by King Sargon of Akkad. About a century later a number of groups of people north and east of Akkad formed a coalition and destroyed this Semitic empire. From about 2070 until 1960 B.C. the Sumerians succeeded in recapturing a goodly portion of their former glory, only to disappear forever as a sovereign people before the onslaughts of several new peoples who arrived from different directions. Chief among these were the Semitic Amorites from western Asia and the Elamites from the region southeast of Mesopotamia. The Amorites increasingly dominated much of western Asia, including Syria and Palestine, and reached the peak of their influence first in Mari on the Middle Euphrates (near the modern Iraq-Syria border) and then in Babylon in the days of Hammurabi (about 1728–1686).

Another important ethnic element in the Fertile Crescent in the first half of the second millennium was the Hurrians (Biblical Horites). Shortly before 2000 B.C. they began to come down in ever-increasing numbers from the mountainous regions northeast of Mesopotamia, and by the end of the fifteenth century they were to be found in every part of western Asia, including Syria and Palestine, in many instances alongside the Amorites. The Hurrians attained their greatest prominence in the Mitanni Kingdom (about 1470–1350 B.C.), which extended from the region east of the upper part of the Tigris to the Mediterranean coast of Syria.

In this period and area, the ethnic group from which the Hebrews of the Bible finally emerged took its place in documented history. The fragmentary data available seems to suggest that various nomadic groups, both Semitic and non-Semitic, but generally known as Habiru, began to appear about 2000 B.C. They wandered from one area to another, sometimes with their own flocks or as skilled craftsmen, smiths, musicians, and the like. At other times they hired themselves out for specific functions and periods of time, for example, as mercenaries and as private or government slaves. Not infrequently they made sudden raids on caravans and on weak, outlying communities, and according to their success either became prisoners of war and state slaves or settled down permanently in conquered towns and regions.

There appears to be good reason for associating the Biblical Hebrews with these far-flung Habiru. Not only does the Biblical account place the career of the Hebrews within the general orbit of the activities of some of the Habiru groups in the different lands of the Near East and in the different epochs of the second millennium B.C., but the term Habiru ceased to occur in extra-Biblical sources at about the same time that the term Hebrew ceased to be used in the Bible. Before the end of the second millennium, those of the Habiru groups which had conquered and become associated with specific territories acquired new, national names, e.g., Moabites, Ammonites, Edomites; the rest of the Habiru had become absorbed by the various settled communities in which they found themselves.

The story of the name "Hebrews" is much the same. Originally associated with some of these widely scattered Habiru groups, the Hebrews of the Bible came in time to lead a career of their own in a specific region, namely Canaan; and the name Hebrews gave way to the name Israelites (literally, "Children of Israel") when the nation came into being. Thus the Biblical term Hebrew was never employed for the nation any more than the term Habiru was.

The Patriarchs in Canaan

Abraham and his immediate descendants and relatives, including his nephew Lot, led a career which was characteristic of those days. They constituted a seminomadic group which settled for a while in a convenient region among the Semitic and non-Semitic (especially Hurrian and Hittite) people of the land, and then, as shepherds, artisans, and merchants, went on to another region. The land of the Canaanites, southern Syria and Palestine, was eminently suited to such free movement at that time. About 1800 B.C. western Palestine and southern Syria were generally occupied by city-states, largely under Egyptian control. Because the lowlands had the best soil and water supply, the cities of Palestine were located mostly along the Mediterranean coastal plain, in the valley of Jezreel (Esdraelon), and in the valley of the Jordan.

Central Palestine, the hilly region between the Jordan Valley and the coastal plain, was only sporadically settled. Though ill suited for agriculture, it was inviting enough to nomads with sheep and goats to graze. And so it was to this hill country, and to the even emptier and drier Negeb below, that Abraham and his family tended. In the Hill Country the patriarchs were associated with such places as Mamre, Bethel, Shechem, and Dothan (Map II). It is now known archaeologically that the last three places existed in this period; and Mamre, it would seem, was employed as the place name in Abraham's time only because the better-known Hebron was not yet founded (about 1700 B.C.).

In the Negeb, Beersheba was the focal point, as it has remained ever since. In Abraham's time Sodom and Gomorrah and other towns in the Vale of Siddim, at the southern end of the Dead Sea, were flourishing, and archaeology supports the Biblical story of their catastrophic end.

The patriarchal seminomadic mode of life required a

relatively simple social structure. The father was the head of the family. The sons and daughters, with their spouses and children, were all subject to the authority of the patriarch. By tribal law, the oldest son succeeded the father upon his death. The tribe lived from its herds and flocks and from the itinerant labor of its craftsmen members—for example, the smiths and musicians.

Two Egyptian sources reproduce extraordinarily well the social atmosphere breathed in Genesis. An Egyptian by the name of Sinuhe tells of his experiences in southern Syria and northern Palestine during the latter half of the twentieth century B.C. He relates, in the "Tale of Sinuhe," how an important Amorite ruler in Syria took him in and married him to his oldest daughter:

He set me at the head of his children. He married me to his eldest daughter. . . . He made me ruler of a tribe of the choicest of the country. Bread was made for me as daily fare, wine as daily provision, cooked meat and roast fowl, beside the wild beasts of the desert, for they hunted for me. . . . I spent many years [there], and my children grew up to be strong men, each man as the chief of his own tribe. The messenger who went north or who went south to the Residence City tarried with me, for I used to make everybody stop over. I gave water to the thirsty. I put him who strayed, [back] on the road. I rescued him who had been robbed. . . . Every foreign country against which I went forth, when I had made my attack on it, was driven away from its pasturage and its wells. I plundered its cattle, carried off its inhabitants, took away their food, and slew people in it.[1]

[1] "The Story of Sinuhe," trans. J. A. Wilson, in *Ancient Near Eastern Texts relating to the Old Testament*, ed. J. B. Pritchard (Princeton, 1950), pp. 18–22.

The other Egyptian source is pictorial. A scene painted about 1900 B.C. on the wall of a noble's tomb at Beni Hasan, on the Nile in Middle Egypt, depicts a family of thirty-seven Semites from western Asia, seminomads come to Egypt to sell stibium, the popular black eye cosmetic. Several elements in the scene are common to the Biblical material. One is reminded of the families of the patriarchs; Jacob's family which went down to Egypt numbered seventy persons, including the children and grandchildren. The clothes are striped lengthwise and very colorful, and recall Joseph's so-called "coat of many colors." The lyre, the javelins, the bows and arrows, and the portable bellows are all characteristic of the occupations of the seminomadic groups. The little donkeys in the scene were the principal means of travel before the domestication of the camel.

The Biblical Cosmogony

All religions have a cosmogony, an explanation of how the world and mankind came to be. The Biblical cosmogony in the Book of Genesis (Chapters 1–11), dealing with Creation, the Garden of Eden (Paradise), the Fall of Man, the antediluvian (pre-Flood) patriarchs, the Flood and Noah's Ark, the Tower of Babel and the dispersion of man over the earth—all these came from the earlier part of the second millennium, when the Hebrews had direct contact with Mesopotamian society. A relationship between the most important Babylonian story of creation, now popularly designated from its first two words, *Enûma Elish* ("When Above"), and the Biblical Genesis has long been recognized. Thus the two share in common the concept of a primeval watery chaos and the subsequent creation of the heaven and the earth. Both accounts speak of the existence of light prior to the creation of the sun, the moon, and the other heavenly bodies, which, in turn, made possible the regulation of time. The Babylonian and the Hebrew versions both regard man as the final and most important act of creation, after which the creators rested. The Bible (Genesis 5) records ten patriarchs from Adam through Noah, who lived a total of 8,575 years, although the actual elapsed time was just over 1,000 years. Methuselah died at the ripest old age of them all, in his 969th year. Yet even these high numbers pale into insignificance in the light of one Sumerian list, which tells of eight antediluvian kings who reigned a total of 241,200 years, and a Babylonian list, compiled in the third century B.C. from much older sources, which records ten such rulers who reigned a total of 432,000 years.

The Biblical account of the Flood, with which God destroyed a world grown wicked, saving only enough of it to make a fresh start, is powerfully foreshadowed in the famous Gilgamesh Epic, which came down to the Babylonians from the earlier Sumerian civilization. Warned by the god Ea, Utnapishtim, the tenth antediluvian king in Babylonia, builds an ark in the shape of a cube, 120 cubits on each side. Into this ship he loads his family, his possessions, and "the seed of all living creatures." The epic relates how

Six days and nights
The wind blew, the downpour, the tempest, the flood overwhelmed the land,
When the seventh day arrived, the tempest, the flood,
Which had fought like an army, subsided in its onslaught.
The sea grew quiet, the storm abated, the flood ceased.
I opened a window, and light fell upon my face.

I looked upon the sea, (all) was silence,
And all mankind had turned to clay.

.   .   .   .   .

On Mount Nisir (or Nimush) the ship landed.
Mount Nisir held the ship fast, and did not let it move.

.   .   .   .   .

When the seventh day arrived,
I sent forth a dove and let her go.
The dove went away and came back to me;
There was no resting-place, and so she returned.
I sent forth a swallow and let her go.
The swallow went away and came back to me;
There was no resting-place, and so she returned.
I sent forth a raven and let her go.
The raven went away, and when she saw that the waters had
    abated,
She ate, she flew about, she cawed, and did not return.
I sent forth (everything) to the four winds and offered a
    sacrifice.
I poured out a libation on the peak of the mountain.[2]

Although the resemblances between the Gilgamesh Epic
and the Biblical account of Noah—who is also the tenth
antediluvian patriarch—are numerous and varied, including
such details as the Ark, the Flood, and the like, the differences are no less notable. It is frequently difficult to determine
precisely what concepts the Hebrews derived from the various milieus in which they found themselves before about
1500 B.C. What is fundamental, however, is that the Hebrews infused whatever concepts they did borrow with their

---

[2] A. Heidel, *The Gilgamesh Epic and Old Testament Parallels*
(Chicago, 1946), pp. 81 ff.

own spirit and thinking, thus endowing them with a content of ethics and morals which lifted the primitive mythology of their Asiatic neighbors to a wholly new spiritual level.

The moral emphasis achieved in the Biblical cosmogony, as contrasted with the naturalism of the prototypes, is sharply illustrated by yet another Babylonian flood legend, the Atrakhasis Epic. Here we are told how

The god [Enlil] became disturbed by their gatherings.
The god heard their noise
And said to the great gods:
"Great has become the noise of mankind;
With their tumult they make sleep impossible."

In other words, the gods are moved to reprisal by simple personal annoyance, whereas in Genesis God's anger is stirred by man's moral decline. As the Bible says: "The Lord saw that the wickedness of man was great in the earth, and that every imagination of the thoughts of his heart was only evil continually" (Genesis 6:5).[3]

The Patriarchal Conception of God and the Covenant

Some features in the patriarchal stage of Israelite history stand out with especial significance. While the picture in detail is still far from clear, the Biblical and the newer archaeological data combine to indicate that the patriarchs practiced a religion which, while not monotheistic in our sense of the term, was yet not polytheistic either.

Its basic concept, later to develop into national significance, was the "covenant." This was the tribal practice of

---

[3] See J. J. Finkelstein, "Bible and Babel," *Commentary*, XXVI (1958), 431–444.

entering into an agreement with one particular god, so that the deity would devote himself entirely to the covenanters, in return for their exclusive obedience and loyal trust. Abraham entered into a mutually exclusive agreement with God, "the God of Abraham," whereby Abraham was to recognize and worship no other deity and God was to protect and seek the welfare of Abraham and his family exclusively. In this regard, the Hebrews went far beyond their Mesopotamian counterparts, where the contractual relationship remained on a purely economic *quid pro quo* basis and the magic element played a most important role.

When Isaac renewed Abraham's covenant, God became "the Kinsman of Isaac." For Jacob, God was "the Champion of Jacob." Abraham's brother, Nahor, the one left behind in Haran, likewise adopted a personal god. When Abraham's grandson Jacob and Nahor's grandson Laban settled a dispute between themselves, Jacob said to Laban, "If the God of my father, the God of Abraham and the Kinsman of Isaac, had not been with me, you would have sent me away empty" (Genesis 31:42). Whereupon Laban answered, "Let the God of Abraham and the God of Nahor, the God of their father, judge between us" (verse 53).

It would be going too far to attribute to the patriarchal Hebrews a belief in the existence of one and only one God. In a sense they may be said to have practiced—but without defining—monotheism. While they probably did not think of denying the existence of other gods, and some mighty ones among them at that, the patriarchs attached themselves to one God, and Him alone they worshiped. With Him, they entered voluntarily into a covenant which was binding forever, never to be broken under penalty of severe punishment and, theoretically at least, even complete rejection. It is not possible to understand the subsequent career of Israel without understanding these two inseparable concepts which arose in patriarchal times: practical monotheism and the personal covenant between the patriarchal families and their God.

The Questioning Spirit

Another phenomenon which apparently struck root in the patriarchal period is the fundamentally questioning and antidogmatic character and outlook of ancient Israel. Within the patriarchal structure, it is true, the patriarch was the chief figure, and no one was free from his final authority. In actual life, however, the matriarch too was a dominant figure, for example, Abraham's wife Sarah and Isaac's wife Rebekkah. And within the household at large there was considerable freedom of action. In the domestic sphere, the woman's ameliorative counsels and her motherly feelings were taken seriously. An important check on patriarchal authority was economically grounded. By custom, the land was regarded as ultimately inalienable, so that family and tribal rather than private rights were the norm.

God, too, was conceived in patriarchal terms, theoretically omnipotent but actually subject to considerable questioning. He was not regarded as a faraway, impersonal deity. The very notion of a covenant implies the equality of the covenanters, and the devotion exacted from God by the patriarchs was no less thorough than that exacted from them by Him. He was near at hand whenever needed, a member of the patriarchal household and available for extended question-and-answer periods. Beginning with the seminomadic family structure of patriarchal society, and down to the time of the composition of the latest books in the Bible, there runs through Hebrew literature the characteristic and persistent feature of questioning authority. The Hebrew mind expressed its deepest self in its opposition to the absolute rule of any one man or tribe, be it kinsman or alien. This attitude extended even to the rule of God. Thus, in the famous dialogue between Abraham and God in Genesis 18:16–33, Abraham flatly objected when God proposed to obliterate Sodom, on the grounds that it was not fair to punish good men along with the bad. And Abraham would not rest content until God promised not to vent His anger, so long as there were as few as ten righteous men left. Which, however, seems not to have been the case.

In this respect, the patriarchal narratives reflected the pattern of contemporaneous Near Eastern saga in which the heroes talked back to the gods.

The Book of Job provides an even more famous example of putting God to the question. But it is worth noting that neither Abraham nor Job partook of the character of a Promethean rebel. They were not insurrectionaries against God; they wanted only to see justice done, to understand God's powers, to have the contract properly drawn up and fulfilled on both sides.

CHAPTER II

Bondage, Exodus, and the National Covenant

THE second important epoch in the career of ancient Israel began with the descent of a group of Hebrews into Egypt sometime around the late seventeenth or early sixteenth century B.C. By the time their descendants had found their way back to Canaan, several centuries later, they were on the verge of nationhood. The Egyptian experience was a decisive factor in the development of Israel as a people. Here the Hebrew families grew in number, and their conception of God and His covenant with them was extended to cover the entire Hebrew folk. Here also they continued to oppose state autocracy, in contrast to the abject submission of the Egyptian people at large. The ancient custom of deifying kings, nowhere more elaborately developed than in Egypt, left them fundamentally untouched. In this great episode, the heroic figure of Moses stands out in epic grandeur.

Eisodus: Egypt and the Hyksos

Whenever a drought and famine desolated the region of Palestine, it was common for whole tribes to pick up their belongings and seek refuge in Egypt. There the periodic overflow of the Nile gave life to the land, as it does today, and helped to regulate the agriculture of the country. The Egyptians learned early to dig channels for the seasonal flood and to irrigate the grain-producing land. Migration into Egypt was therefore an ancient expedient.

In Palestine, on the other hand, the rains did not always come when needed. A late-thirteenth-century Egyptian document, for example, tells how the seminomadic inhabitants of Edom, south of Palestine, left their homes in time of drought to come to Egypt "to keep themselves alive and to keep their cattle alive." It was famine, too, as the Bible says, which compelled Abraham and Isaac in an earlier period to go south (Genesis 12 and 26), and the same reason is given for Jacob's sending his sons to Egypt, where grain could still be procured even in a time of general drought (Genesis 42 ff.). As a result of this mission, the entire family finally settled there.

At the same time, this Eisodus—the "going into," as distinguished from the Exodus, the "going out of"—may also have been encouraged by certain ethnic disturbances which for a period disrupted Egyptian suzerainty in Canaan and reduced the sovereignty of the Egyptian homeland as well. Following upon the increasing disintegration of the Egyptian state, a mixed group of Asiatics, apparently mostly Semites, and known generally as Hyksos (literally, "rulers of foreign countries"), appeared in the north and swarmed down through Syria and Palestine. By about 1720 B.C. they had crossed the land bridge into Africa and conquered much of Egypt, a domination that was not to be completely broken until about 1550.

Between the Hyksos and the Hebrews there appear to be a number of points of contact. It is known, for instance, that a certain Hyksos chieftain in Egypt bore the name Jacob-el, or perhaps Jacob-har, which means "May El, or Har [the mountain god] Give Protection." Another Hyksos leader was called Jacob-baal, "May Baal Protect." The verbal element, Jacob, which means "protect," is identical with the name of the Hebrew patriarch Jacob who settled in Egypt. Again, the historical kernel which resides in the dramatic story of the career of Joseph in Egypt, of the coming to power of a Hebrew in the Egyptian court, could well have derived from the period of the Hyksos, when Semites, and in all probability Habiru among them, were prominent among the new rulers of Egypt. For it was not Egyptian habit to nourish the ambitions of strangers in their midst. Furthermore, it would seem to be more than a mere coincidence that the Hebrews, according to the Bible, settled in Goshen in the Delta, the very area which the Hyksos built up around their new capital Avaris, the later Tanis.

In this connection it is also interesting to note that Josephus, the Jewish historian of the first century A.D., quotes the Egyptian historian Manetho (about 275 B.C.), to the effect that a large number of Hyksos made their way from Avaris to Canaan and there built Jerusalem. These Hyksos, according to Manetho, were "not fewer in number than 240,000," a figure which recalls the Biblical statement (Numbers 1:46) that 603,550 Hebrew males, exclusive of Levites, women, and children, participated in the Exodus from Egypt.

All these facts suggest that the Hebrews and the Hyksos

may have been on terms of considerable intimacy; so that the entry of the Hebrews into Egypt would have been facilitated by the presence of Hyksos in positions of power, and the Bondage accounted for by the enslavement of foreign elements after the fall of the Hyksos invaders. If this hypothesis be accepted, it provides evidence that the Biblical version of the Hebrew sojourn in Egypt (Genesis 39–50; Exodus 1 ff.) derives from the same period as the events which it describes. For the Egyptians themselves, humiliated by their conquest at the hands of the Hyksos, avoided and suppressed any reference to the events of the period, and it would have been well-nigh impossible for anyone to learn the historical details very much later.

The Sojourn

The Bible itself elaborates only on the final period of the Bondage in Egypt. But what was there to say? After the Egyptians had overthrown the Hyksos, they enslaved those foreigners who had not fled, thus reversing the status of the non-Egyptians in the land as the Bible records: "And a new king arose in Egypt who did not know Joseph. . . . And they [the Egyptians] set taskmasters over them [the Hebrews] to oppress them with forced labor. And they built for Pharaoh store-cities, Pithom and Ramses" (Exodus 1:8–11).

Under the Hyksos domination, Egyptian culture had sunk so low that the period has been described as "The Great Humiliation." But the successful war of liberation against the Hyksos led to an Egyptian revival on such a grand scale that the period of the New Kingdom which followed, especially during the Eighteenth and Nineteenth Dynasties (about 1550–1150), has been called the Golden Age and was the subject of a recent book which bore the suggestive title, *When Egypt Ruled the East*.[1] The development of literature, art, and building, the inculcation of individual physical prowess in sport and in battle, the marked extension of the influence of women in the royal court and in upper-class circles generally—all of these manifested a new cosmopolitanism, and even secularism, brought on by imperial expansion abroad and urbanization at home.

There was much in the Egyptian environment that the Hebrews could emulate. But the kind of life which they and others led in the Egyptian slave camps did not encourage cultural apprenticeship. "Slave troops on a government building project," as one authority puts it, "have no opportunity for discussion with priests and scribes. Their simple desert souls would see and shrink from some of the abominations of the effete civilization and long to escape dreary enslavement rather than admire the cultural triumph of the land of bondage."[2]

Moses, Leader of the Exodus

It was probably sometime in the thirteenth century that a group of Hebrews and others united under the leadership of Moses, of the tribe of Levi, to escape from Egypt. This tribe was foremost in organizing those state slaves who were willing to chance the break for freedom. Several outstanding Levites bore Egyptian names, for example, Moses, Miriam, Hophni, Phinehas, Merari, Puti-el, and perhaps Aaron. This alone indicates a considerable period of residence in Egypt; also a surprising degree of resistance and determination to be free, despite a long period of slavery.

---

[1] G. Steindorff and K. C. Seele, *When Egypt Ruled the East*, rev. ed. (Chicago, 1957).

[2] J. A. Wilson, *The Burden of Egypt* (Chicago, 1951), p. 256.

The Bible makes it amply clear that some non-Hebrew elements, "the mixed multitude" of Exodus (12:38) and Numbers (11:4), accompanied Moses and the Hebrews out of Egypt. The Egyptian sources, in turn, provide a very clear background for this circumstance. Tens of thousands of workers, natives of many countries and members of different ethnic groups, labored for the Egyptian state. Already in the fifteenth century, as a result of the military conquests of Amenhotep II in Syria and Palestine, large numbers of Semitic and non-Semitic captives of war, including 3,600 Apiru (Habiru), were brought to Egypt as state slaves. The military campaigns of other Egyptian kings, from the fourteenth to the twelfth centuries, produced similar results. The great building projects of Ramses II (about 1301–1234), at such places at Pithom and Ramses, employed these "mixed multitudes," many of whom were eager to escape from slavery.

Scholars have long been troubled by the fact that Egyptian records make no mention of Moses and the Exodus, and some have expressed the belief that a document or two may yet turn up with reference to them. Yet the modern student of ancient Egyptian history should share neither this worry nor this optimism. First, when the Egyptians lost a battle, they customarily either recorded it as a victory or else passed over it in silence. Thus the prolonged Hyksos rule was not mentioned in contemporaneous Egyptian sources until the Hyksos were expelled, and even the victory over them was apparently not officially recorded. And second, the scope of the Exodus and significance of it for the Egyptian government were so meager as not to merit any documentary mention.

The Wandering in the Wilderness

The peninsula of Sinai is a smaller replica of the Arabian peninsula, which lies farther east and south of it. On the west, Sinai is bounded by a deep-reaching arm of the Red Sea, and on the east by the Gulf of Aqabah, as the Persian Gulf forms the eastern boundary of the Arabian peninsula. It was into this burning desert upland that Moses led the way.

Here, in the wilderness of Sinai, Israel was forged, hammered into shape amid appalling hardship. The weak and weary perished, leaving the young and strong to drift yet another mile toward the Land of Promise, the ancestral home.

There was endless and violent struggle for power within this group that Moses had led from Egypt. Korah and his faction of Levites and Reubenites challenged the authority of Moses himself (Numbers 16). Aaron, in the incident of the Golden Calf, was used by another faction in a similar struggle (Exodus 32). There was the additional difficulty that the "mixed multitude" reminded themselves in the wilderness of Sinai of "the fish which we used to eat in Egypt free; the cucumbers, the melons, the leeks, the onions, and the garlic; but now our appetite is starved!" (Numbers 11:4–5). Only a man of iron will could have endured this endless bickering, scheming, and backsliding. Moses was that man.

It was in the wilderness of Sinai, and not in Egypt or Canaan, that this struggle for power took place, and the subsequent welding together of a heterogeneous, inexperienced, and uncultured mass of individuals into something of a unified force and social group. That about a generation

—the traditional "forty years" of wandering—should have elapsed before the goal was approached is not only reasonable, but also accounts for the fact that virtually none of the leaders of the Exodus, such as Moses, Aaron, and Miriam, lived to enter the Promised Land.

Until recently the Bible has been virtually the only source for the history of the wandering in the Wilderness. As a result, the significance of this stage in Israel's history has been minimized, when its very authenticity has not been questioned.

A central feature of the Biblical account is the movable Tabernacle, or Tent of Meeting, around which the political and religious life of the wandering Hebrews revolved. This institution used to be regarded as a late fiction, projected back into the past. Recently, however, archaeological and literary parallels have been accumulating which not only explain the origin of this structure and institution in the wilderness of Sinai, but also clarify its history as the "Tent of the Lord" at Shiloh, following the conquest of Canaan. It was ultimately replaced by the Temple which David planned and Solomon built.

Much the same thing happened in the case of the Ark, the acacia chest in which, according to tradition, Moses placed and kept the two stone tablets recording the Ten Commandments. Furthermore, the traditional route of the Wandering, as described in the books of Exodus and Numbers, accords well with the topography of Sinai and with what has been learned of the location of the copper and turquoise mines which were being worked and garrisoned in the thirteenth century B.C. These garrisoned sites, in the hands of the Egyptians, appear to have been situated at just those points which the Hebrews were careful to avoid in their trek through Sinai.

Moses and the Covenant

The Covenant between God and the new nation, a factor of fundamental importance in Israel's career, came into being during this period. The relationship between the patriarchs and their God had begun, according to the social patterns of seminomadic family life, as a personal arrangement. In Moses' first experience with the Deity, at the theophany in the burning bush (Exodus 3), the relationship was also personal; and in accord with the patriarchal tradition, the Deity Himself acquired a new personal name, YHWH, which is usually rendered "Lord" or "Jehovah." [3]

The experiences of the Exodus and the Wandering gradually forged the more individualistic elements into the new tribal or national unit. The purpose of the Exodus was not merely to free a group of slaves for their own sakes, but for something far greater in scope and significance, the creation

[3] The Hebrew term consists of four letters, YHWH, and hence is called the Tetragrammaton. Some time after about the fifth century B.C., the original pronunciation of the name ceased to be employed for ordinary purposes, and the term Adonai, "Lord," came to be substituted for it. The term Jehovah is a relatively recent creation (about fourteenth century A.D.), by a Christian who erroneously read the vowels of Adonai together with the consonants of YHWH. The Revised Standard Version (New York, 1952) follows the tradition of the King James (so-called Authorized) Version, the Revised Version, and the Jewish Publication Society Translation in rejecting the term Jehovah, usually in favor of Lord.

Many scholars believe that the original pronunciation of YHWH was Yahweh. The evidence for this belief, however, is not decisive, and there are also very considerable differences of opinion as to what the term meant originally.

of a new nation. The direct relationship between God and the Nation was the new element created by the forces of history and circumstance. From that point on, and throughout the entire Bible henceforth, the new Covenant, a national pact between God and His people, sealed by the act of the Exodus, replaced the older, individual covenants between God and the patriarchal leaders.

The personality of Moses so dominated Israel's formative years that later centuries came to credit him with authorship of the Pentateuch. This honor is more than justified in a figurative sense, and perhaps even in a factual sense as well. Research has now shown that an important part of the legal code of ancient Israel clearly derives from the pre-Canaanite period which coincides with the Hebrew wandering in the Wilderness (see below in Chapter III). And the Sinaitic origin of the Tabernacle, noted above, implies the development of numerous religious and cultic regulations under the leadership of Moses.

Great intelligence and character were required to solve the many vexing problems, to take advantage fully and wisely of the new and changing circumstances, to know when to follow and when to lead the unorganized Hebrews and their fellow travelers. When the mixed tribal following had emerged from the wilderness, they were all bound to one God. Moses alone provided that essential leadership, and he well deserves his traditional reputation of having brought Israel into being as a nation.

The question of who would succeed Moses in authority was of prime importance; there appears to have been no opposition to Moses' selection of Joshua of the tribe of Ephraim as his successor.

Moses and the Atonism of Akh-en-aton

According to a much-quoted theory, Moses could have acquired the concept of monotheism which he introduced to the Hebrews only from the Egyptian environment in which he had grown up, specifically from the so-called monotheism of the Aton. This worship of the round disk of the sun, while known previously in Egypt, found an ardent devotee in Amenhotep IV (Akh-en-aton; about 1380–1362 B.C.).

Two important facts, however, each independent of the other, disprove this theory. First, Moses could hardly have been affected by Atonism, since this worship was limited to Akh-en-aton and his family and was crushed immediately after Akh-en-aton's death. Indeed, Akh-en-aton's own couriers had worshiped Akh-en-aton himself; and Atonism itself was not truly monotheistic. Second, in sponsoring monotheism, Moses was actually not introducing a new concept to the Hebrews. He had a familiar, developable Hebraic idea of monotheism to work with, and even the Covenant of Sinai represented not so much a change in kind as a change in degree from the old way of binding oneself to the Deity.

Finally, the Bible makes it clear that the Hebrews brought with them from Egypt little or no cultural baggage.

CHAPTER III

Israel in Canaan:

The Period of the Judges

CANAAN was the home of the patriarchs, and it was with this land that the God of the patriarchs was associated. Moses and all later leaders recognized this fundamental fact, and it was to Canaan that they led the Hebrews through the wilderness. During the period of the Judges, in the twelfth and eleventh centuries, when the term "Israelites" replaced that of "Hebrews," the relationship of God, Israel, and the Land of Israel became intertwined and indissoluble, as it has remained ever after. In the view of the Biblical writers there could have been no Israel without God and the Holy Land.

The Geography of the Land of Israel

Palestine covers approximately 10,000 square miles spread over an area that stretches from Dan in the north, at the foot of the Anti-Lebanon mountain range, to below Beersheba in the south, and from the Mediterranean Sea in the west to the desert fringes of Transjordan in the east. (See Map II.) The whole territory, of which about three-fifths lies west of the Jordan, resembles in size and shape the state

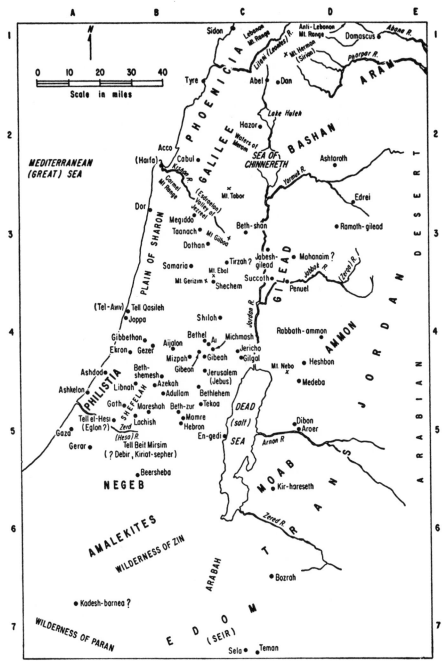

II. Israel in the period of the judges and kings (about 1200–600 B.C.).

of New Hampshire. This little country is broken up into some eight natural geographical units.

First there is the coastal plain along the Mediterranean, about ten miles wide and divided in half approximately at Joppa, near modern Tel Aviv. The Plain of Sharon lies to the north as far as the Carmel range near modern Haifa, and the more important Philistine plain, Philistia, lies to the south. The Plain of Acco extends north of Sharon, from the Carmel mountains to Acco and somewhat beyond. Further along the coast lay Phoenicia, separated from Acco and the rest of western Palestine by mountains of the region.

To the east of and paralleling Philistia rises the Shefelah, the second principal area, which is separated by longitudinal valleys from the central Hill Country and forms the transition to it. The Hill Country begins in southern Syria and in the form of hills and mountains extends down the length of Palestine until it begins to peter out in the extreme south.

The third part, the northern Hill Country, is called Galilee, and is usually subdivided into Upper and Lower Galilee. The fourth unit is the Valley of Jezreel, or Esdraelon (or simply "The Valley"), which cuts right across Galilee and constitutes the easy road for traders and invaders to reach Transjordan. Central Palestine, the fifth part, consisted of Samaria in the north, with the southern sector constituting Judah. The sixth division, formed by the rest of western Palestine, was the vast semiarid area in the south, the Negeb.

The territory west of the Jordan, the seventh section, was separated from Transjordan by a geologically marvelous "rift valley," the corollary of the long range of hills which forms the Hill Country. This rift begins in Syria, separates and forms Mount Lebanon and Mount Anti-Lebanon (Biblical Hermon), and continues south in the form of the Jordan Valley and the Arabah, to the Gulf of Aqabah and the Red Sea—indeed, as far as Mozambique and into the great depressions filled by the African lakes. The Jordan River runs through the valley, pooled en route in Lake Huleh and the Sea of Galilee (or Chinnereth), and terminates to the south in the cul-de-sac which is the Dead, or Salt, Sea. The last two bodies of water fill below-sea-level troughs in the valley floor. The Dead Sea, about 1,275 feet below the Mediterranean, is the lowest depression in the world.

Finally, eastern Palestine, or Transjordan, is essentially a plateau, and is divided up by four rivers into five main regions. The Yarmuk River, flowing into the Jordan just south of the Sea of Galilee, made up the dividing line between Bashan and Gilead. The Jabbok, or Wadi Zerqa, emptying into the Jordan about two-thirds of the way down, constituted the boundary between Gilead and Ammon. The Arnon, or Wadi Mojib, in turn, sometimes served as the natural barrier between Ammon and Moab, at the middle of the Dead Sea. The boundary between the two countries varied during Biblical times, usually lying north of the Arnon. Finally, at the southern end of the Dead Sea, the Zered, or Wadi Hesa, separated Moab from Edom. When it rained, these wadies became real streams. Otherwise they were mostly dry riverbeds.

The Climate of the Holy Land

Small as it is, Palestine has always had the advantages of many kinds of climate, owing in part to the variety of the terrain. In general, the land resembles the drier parts of

Southern California, but everything is on a much smaller scale. Mount Hermon in the north, which is over 9,000 feet high, tends to be cold, whereas just over one hundred miles to the south, in the Jordan Valley, Jericho swelters in tropical heat. Jerusalem, although less than fifteen miles to the southwest of Jericho, is almost 4,000 feet higher, and its inhabitants have usually found its climate temperate.

From Jerusalem to the coast the distance is just over thirty miles, and the descent from about 2,600 feet to sea level. The coastal climate is of course much warmer, although never so unbearable in summer as the Jordan Valley. The temperatures in the Transjordan plateau approximate those of Jerusalem.

There is another important element, the winds. The winds from the east are usually hot and dry, coming as they do from the desert. Those from the north, on the other hand, and especially from the west across the Mediterranean, are much more gentle, bringing with them cool air and rain. The all-important rainy season usually begins in October and ends in March or April. One of God's greatest blessings to Israel was His promise: "I will give the rain of your land in its season, the former rain and the latter rain, that you may gather in your new grain, wine, and oil" (Deuteronomy 11:14; 28:12). The threat of drought was a curse and a disaster (28:23–24).

Geography and Economy

A network of valleys provided avenues of settlement as well as commercial and military traffic. This made for the historical interplay between hill and valley peoples that figures so prominently in the books of Joshua, Judges, and Samuel.

Geography made Biblical Israel primarily an agricultural, and only secondarily a commercial, society. The coastal plains of Sharon and Philistia, the Jezreel and Jordan valleys, and a considerable part of the Hill Country of Samaria and Judah lent themselves to successful farming. Even the nearly waterless Negeb was tilled profitably when the inhabitants diligently exploited the available supply of water by terracing and irrigating the land.

Ancient Israel, with its few and inadequate harbors, derived slight commercial advantage from its Mediterranean coast. Even Dor and Joppa, the nation's best ports, could be used only when the sea was calm. Such better harbors as were to be found along the coast, Byblos, Sidon, Tyre, and usually even Acco, were in Phoenician hands. In the days of Solomon, considerable maritime trade centered about Ezion-geber and Elath on the Gulf of Aqabah and continued at least sporadically for some time after his reign.

It was as the bridge between Asia and Africa that the land of Israel acquired commercial significance. Its plains and valleys, notably Jezreel and the Mediterranean coast, were commercial and military highways from time immemorial; and this fact explains why the sites which guarded and controlled these routes played so important a role in Biblical history. Beth-shan, Megiddo, Shechem, Gaza, and Beersheba were among the better-known cities in the west, and in Transjordan such sites as Ashtaroth, Ramoth-gilead, Rabbath-ammon, Heshbon, and Kir-hareseth dominated the main road from Damascus through Bashan, Gilead, Ammon, and Moab, to Edom in the south.

Israel was not rich in natural resources. The copper and iron ores in the south were exploited by the Israelites only when Edom was under their control. Limited both in area and water supply, the country could not support a large population; but in spite of that the Israelites might well have succeeded in turning their domain into "a land flowing with milk and honey" (Exodus 3:8) if it had not fallen directly across the path of invasion and conquest followed by the expanding empires of western Asia and Egypt.

Joshua and the Conquest of Canaan: The Ideal and the Reality

According to the traditional understanding of the Biblical account, the taking of Canaan was accomplished in a single spectacularly successful invasion, with Joshua smiting one-and-thirty kings. In this picture, the Hebrew tribes, led by Joshua, crossed the Jordan near the Dead Sea and took the key point of Jericho, "whose walls came tumbling down." The next objective was Ai, up in the Hill Country, just over ten miles west of Jericho as the crow flies, but twice as far by foot. This fortified place Joshua took by strategem.

Thereafter, in a series of forays down the valleys—on one occasion, the lost Book of Jashar tells us (Joshua 10:12–14), he commanded the sun in Gibeon and the moon in the valley of Aijalon to stand still, so that he could mop up remnants of Canaanite resistance—Joshua took and razed a series of fortified towns, Libnah, Lachish, Eglon, Hebron, and Debir. This done, he conquered all the highland of southern Canaan, a section of the coastal strip as far as Gaza, and then in the north by the Waters of Merom, a hundred miles more or less from his base at Gilgal, he routed a Canaanite army.

Reuben, Gad, and half of the tribe of Manasseh occupied Transjordan; the other half of Manasseh settled on the

Plain of Sharon just south of Esdraelon. The tribe of Levi, consisting entirely of religious functionaries, received no single fixed territory. The rest of the tribes shared in the partition of Canaan according to their population.

The author of Chapters 10–11 in the Book of Joshua provides the basis for this traditional view. Joshua, he recounts,

defeated all the land, the hill country, and the Negeb, and the Shefelah, and the slopes, and all their kings; he left none remaining, but utterly destroyed all that breathed. . . . So Joshua took the whole land, according to all that the Lord said to Moses; and Joshua gave it for an inheritance to Israel according to their divisions by their tribes. And the land had rest from war.

Chapters 15–19 in Joshua and Chapter 1 in Judges, however, give a different picture both of the conquest and of the role of Joshua therein. This version describes the conquest as a slow piecemeal affair, accomplished largely after Joshua and his generation were gone, by individual tribes and clans seldom acting even in partial unison. Thus Judges 1:1 would indicate that the land was not at rest from war, in fact was never pacified: "After the death of Joshua, the Israelites asked of the Lord, 'Who shall lead us in battle against the Canaanites?'"

The latter picture of the conquest was generally taken by scholars to be correct and the former thrown into discard, together with Joshua's traditional career, as myth. The truth of the matter, however, appears to comprehend both versions. Excavations at Lachish, Tell Beit Mirsim (= Kiriat-sepher?), Gibeon, Hazor, Eglon, Beth-shemesh, Gibeah, Bethel, Shiloh, Megiddo, and Beth-shan, indicate that these places were destroyed or occupied, then were sometimes retaken and rebuilt by the Canaanites, only to change hands again, during the thirteenth, twelfth, and eleventh centuries B.C. The Biblical version of the Joshuan conquest would seem to be

a collection of miscellaneous fragments *of varying dates and of varying reliability.* . . . There was a campaign by Joshua which achieved an amazing success in attacking certain key Canaanite royal cities but . . . there was also a long period of struggle for possession which continued after Joshua's death.[1]

Biblical authors tended to telescope accounts of long campaigns—a device by no means abandoned even today —and to give all the credit for victory to well-established military heroes such as Joshua. Their purpose, after all, was not merely to chronicle but to dramatize the past and to edify their readers. To achieve this end they naturally tended to lump weary details under one splendid name. Thus Joshua acquires once again an association with the conquest of Canaan no less deserving and prominent in its way than that of Moses with the Exodus and the Wandering.

The Canaanite Civilization

When the Hebrews and Israelites entered Canaan, they found there a highly developed and sophisticated society. Thanks to recent discoveries of inscriptions and other archaeological evidence, part of this highly significant culture has been recovered. Indeed, the Canaanite civilization was so advanced that it nearly absorbed the desert

---

[1] Quoted from G. E. Wright, in *Journal of Near Eastern Studies,* V (1946), 105–114. Joshua's capture of Ai was probably confused with that of Bethel. The archaeological story of Jericho is not clear.

invaders. Thus it was when the Semitic Akkadians swept into the non-Semitic society of Sumer. Thus, too, when Rome conquered Greece, the victors were in turn conquered by the superior culture of their victims.

There can be no doubt that the Israelites of Joshua and Judges were quite unable to match the material techniques of Canaan, at least until the period of Solomon in the tenth century. Israelite fortifications, Saul's strong point at Gibeah for example, did not compare with those of contemporary Canaan. The foundations and masonry found in Canaanite towns are clearly superior to Israelite remains. Canaanite Bethel had a drainage system, which was unknown in Israelite towns. Canaanite pottery of the Middle and Late Bronze Ages (about 2000–1200 B.C.) compared with the best, but the products of Israel were crude.

The origin of the alphabet cannot as yet be determined with precision. But it is the Canaanites, who may well have been associated with its invention, who gave this great cultural force to the world at large. It is likewise uncertain exactly what Semitic language or languages the Hebrews and Israelites spoke in the patriarchal period; but after they settled in Canaan, they adopted a variety of Canaanite alphabets and dialects. For good reason, then, the Bible itself calls the Hebrew language "the tongue of Canaan" (Isaiah 19:18), recognizing Biblical Hebrew as originally a dialect of Canaanite.

Canaanite literature was notable for its mythological and religious compositions. The Greeks and Romans owed much more than their alphabet to the Canaanites, whom the Greeks began to call Phoenicians after 1000 B.C.; they derived also considerable and important elements in their mythologies from them.

The religious system was a highly organized and central element in every aspect of the daily life of the Canaanites, and its influence extended widely into the economic, political, and social spheres. The priests constituted an important and powerful group in the upper class of Canaanite society. They were landowners, slaveowners, and moneylenders on a large scale, operating within the temples and under the protection of the gods. In Canaan, though on a smaller scale than in Mesopotamia and Egypt, the temples "were heavily endowed with landed properties and received a tremendous income. At certain periods they probably owned nearly all the land of the country and acquired almost an economic strangle-hold over the people." [2]

The religious beliefs and practices of the Canaanites revolved about the predominantly agricultural character of their economy. The Canaanites were polytheists, regarding the forces of nature as divine beings and giving to them personal names. These deities personified the heavenly bodies—the sun, moon, stars, and planets—and such manifestations of nature as rain, thunder, lightning, vegetation, death, and wisdom—the last mentioned including the arts and inventions.

Mythological stories and qualities were woven about the careers of the gods, and much of the ritual at the shrines of Canaanite cults was intended primarily to ensure the fertility of the soil. Foremost among the gods was Baal, to whom there is so much derogatory reference in the Bible. The Canaanite Baal was a god of rain, prime mover of the agricultural world. Periodically Baal was killed by the

[2] From a symposium on "The Significance of the Temple in the Ancient Near East," *Biblical Archaeologist*, VII (Sept. and Dec., 1944), 41–88.

forces of Mot, the god of drought and death, so that the rains and vegetation ceased. However, Baal came to life in the fall, and the all-important rains came down again. In the spring Baal and his half-sister Anath, goddess of fertility and war, cohabited, so that fecundity came to the land and its inhabitants. The Canaanite worship of their gods was characterized by idolatry and sexual rites.

Israel and Canaan

The manner in which the Israelites reacted to the Canaanite civilization forms one of the vivid periods in their dramatic career. It will be remembered that not all the Hebrews left Canaan for Egypt in the days of Jacob and Joseph. The stay-at-homes inclined to feel indifferent about a Bondage and Exodus in which their own ancestors had not participated. While their kinsmen had been off adventuring and finding God, they themselves had acquired land, herds, and status. And to this end they had compromised, in great measure or small, with the culture and religion of Canaan. Not for them the harsh dedications of the Law, the admonition from on high,

Be very strong and courageous, being mindful to do according to all the Law which Moses My servant commanded you. . . . This book of the Law shall not depart out of your mouth, but you shall meditate on it day and night . . . for then you shall make your way prosperous, and you shall have good success [Joshua 1:7–8].

These people had already feathered their nests without the assistance of the national Covenant.

Among the new settlers too there developed different points of view. Some of those fresh from the Mosaic scene, once they were comfortably ensconced, found it desirable to wink an eye and look away from the Law. On several occasions the tribes of Reuben and Gad and the half-tribe of Manasseh had to be ordered to help their fellow tribesmen secure their allotments in western Palestine (Joshua 1:12–18). When the crucial struggle between the Israelites and the Canaanites came to a head in the battle near Taanach in the valley of Jezreel (about 1125 B.C.), an event made famous by the triumphal Song of Deborah (Judges 5), several tribes refused to join in the battle and accordingly were cursed. A whole century of indecision and wavering passed before the reluctant tribes, faced with a common danger, were able to bring themselves to make a common cause. The individualism and desert ways of these tribes died hard.

The same process is reflected in the religious picture painted in the Book of Judges. The complete devotion to the Lord advocated by Moses and Joshua ran into dire opposition. The Israelite population at large, even the newcomers in the land, conveniently adapted their way of life to the Canaanite practices, especially those which were aimed at the maintenance and improvement of their well-being. Local shrines, presided over by guilds of priests and seers, sprang up everywhere. While they did not go so far as to produce idols to represent the Lord, many Israelites did acquire figurines of the Canaanite goddess of fertility. They also added to the worship of the Lord ritualistic features from the cults of Baal, Asherah, Ashtoreth, and the other gods of Canaan. In spite of this, the God of Israel survived through thick and thin, even when His influence was diluted by alien admixture. Such heroes as Saul and David (about 1000 B.C.), it should be noted, gave some of their children names which included the element "Baal."

But some, the Gideons of Israel, would not take the pagan bait. At the behest of the Lord, the Bible tells us in Judges 6, Gideon risked his life in the dark of the night by smashing a Baal altar and cutting down the Asherah beside it for firewood for burning an Israelite sacrificial bull. "And when the men of the town rose early in the morning," the account continues, "behold, the altar of Baal was torn down, the sacred pole that was beside it was cut down, and the second bull was offered [to the Lord] upon the altar which had been built" (verse 28).

The authors of the Book of Judges openly blamed Israel's misfortunes during the period of settlement upon this widespread religious defection. When Midianite camel raiders and the better-organized forces of Ammon and Moab overran Israelite communities, their depredations were explained as punishment for Israel's desertion of the Lord. Israel would not have experienced these sufferings, the Biblical writers maintained (Judges 2:11 ff.), if she had held together under the Covenant. Israel's strength lay in united devotion to the Lord, and the worship of Baal was the most divisive and destructive force that Israel had to face. It threatened to destroy the Covenant between God and His chosen people.

The "Judges"

The period from Joshua to King Saul is described in the Bible as "the days when the judges ruled." These "judges" were primarily local military heroes and dominated Israel during the period of pacification and adjustment. When an

alien force attacked a segment of Israel, men of uncommon
mettle frequently stepped forward from among the people
to rally and lead their fellows. Such natural leaders, if they
proved successful, became chieftains and were accepted as
rulers within the area of resistance (Judges 2:14 ff.).

The Bible records some twelve judges in all, some of
them contemporaries, as in the case of Ehud and Shamgar.
The most famous judges were Ehud, Gideon, Jephthah, and
Samson. These successful military chieftains acquired judicial authority, alongside the priests of the local sanctuaries, but only secondarily, and they held it only so long
as "the land had rest" from the enemy. Unlike the judges
of the later monarchy, these "judges" were brought into
being by external, military needs.

Not more than three leaders in the Period of the Judges
really adjudicated; they were Deborah, Eli, and Samuel.
Eli, however, was specifically a priest. And Deborah and
Samuel, unlike the others, are described as "prophets"; indeed, neither one ever served as military leader for any of
the tribes.

Tribal Structure of Israel and her Neighbors

Except for occasional brief emergency alliances, the
Israelite tribes maintained complete autonomy during the
Period of the Judges and recognized no central capital or
shrine for all Israel. "In those days there was no king in
Israel, every man did what was right in his own eyes"
(Judges 17:6, 21:25). The hilly terrain, netted by a maze
of valleys and wadies, made for political disjunction. Since
no enemy was powerful enough to threaten more than a
small part of Israel at any one time, the pressure from without was not great enough to produce any effective integra-

tion. Dwellers on the plains ignored the plight of the hill people, who returned the compliment. An intertribal warfare itself was not unknown, despite a common religion (Judges 12:19–21).

Israelite Economy and Government

The Israelites, meanwhile, raised cattle, sheep, and goats and tilled the soil. Artisans organized guilds, practiced weaving, dyeing, tanning, smithing, pottery making, and other crafts, even though on a very small scale. Private ownership of land, including wells, gradually replaced the communal ownership of patriarchal days.

Even though there was a concentration of wealth among the Canaanites, rich families among the Israelites did not appear to dominate the communities in the time of the judges. Imposing palaces and elaborate fortifications discovered in the Canaanite levels of Palestinian mounds are not equaled in the Israelite levels until the days of Solomon. The lack of concentrated wealth also helped hold back the development of a nationally conscious leadership. This circumstance accounts also for the absence from Israel, at least up to the time of David, of the *corvée*, or forced labor.

During the Period of the Judges there does not appear to have been any centralized authority within the tribal unit capable of dominating the rest of the population. The heads of wealthy and important families constituted a group of "elders," and they met—usually in the town gate, the common meeting place in those days—whenever the occasion demanded. In conjunction with the elders, although the precise relationship remains obscure, there also functioned a public assembly of all the free adult males of the community. The elders and the assembly made their authority felt in every aspect of the community's activities, the military, political, religious, economic, legal, and social. In Israelite society it was not easy to separate the religious from the secular aspects of these activities.

Israel's Legal Codes

During the Period of the Judges the legal system of Israel began to take on definite shape. It is now generally agreed that the legal enactments in the Pentateuch fall into two main groups. Numerous laws are introduced by a direct command or prohibition of the Lord, "You shall (or, shall not). . . ." The Ten Commandments (Exodus 20:1–17) are a case in point, e.g., "You shall have no other gods beside Me," etc. Laws expressed so dogmatically and directly are called *apodictic*.

The second major group of laws, called *casuistic*, is characterized by a conditional clause ("if; provided that"). The Book of the Covenant (Exodus 20:22–23:33; 24:7) is a good example of this formulation, e.g., "If a thief is found breaking in, and he is struck and dies, there shall be no bloodguilt for him" (22:1). Or,

If a foreigner resides with you in your land, you shall not wrong him. The foreigner who resides with you shall be to you as one of your own native born; you shall love him as one of your own; for you were foreigners in the land of Egypt. I am the Lord your God [Leviticus 19:33–4].

In general, Israelite civil law was expressed casuistically, and the ritual law apodictically.

It would seem that the Israelites borrowed to some extent from the legal codes of the Babylonians, Hurrians, and Canaanites. This is apparent especially in the casuistic group of laws. The apodictic group derived primarily from their own experiences in their nomadic wanderings in Canaan and in the wilderness of Sinai. By and large, the Israelites made and compiled their own laws to suit their own way of life, and what they did borrow from others they adapted to their own needs.

The Philistines

About 1175 B.C. a number of Aegean peoples were driven by northern invaders from their homes on Crete and the shores of Asia Minor and took to the sea. They failed to penetrate Egypt, but they did gain a hold on the Palestinian coast. These "sea peoples," as the Egyptians called them, had a superior military and political organization. Despite their lack of numbers, they gradually got a grip on the coastal plain. Among these migrant sea peoples were the Philistines. Indeed, it is from them that the name "Palestine" derives, by way of the Latinized Greek word "Palaestina," as finally impressed on the whole region by the Roman conquerors of Judah over a thousand years later.

Their closely knit political structure, coupled with the need for mercantile expansion, brought the Philistines into the hinterland. Philistine society was divided up into five important city-states, with a "tyrant," or chieftain, at the head of each. These city-states knew how to combine for military attack. Moreover, the Philistines had a virtual monopoly on the important new metal, iron, and used it for swords, ax heads, and chariots, as well as for plough tips and sickles.

The Israelites were squarely in the path of the Philistine drive to the east. Various Israelite tribes were badly hit by the systematic depredations of the strangers from the coast. Eventually the situation reached such a pass that the tribes most seriously affected were driven to submit to a central authority. This novelty, however, was not introduced without bitter resistance from diehards who maintained an extremely literal interpretation of the meaning of the Sinaitic Covenant. The man chosen to be "king" was Saul; the opposition to him was led by Samuel, the priestly seer.

King Saul

Speaking before the elders and assembled freemen, Samuel argued that if they elected Saul to be their king they would be flouting the primacy of God. It was not his own judgeship that he was worrying about, Samuel insisted, but the judgeship of the Lord. In addition he warned the Israelites that a king would take their sons and daughters, the best of their fields, and one-tenth of their seed and flocks. The Israelites, he said, would become the king's servants, which, in effect, meant his slaves. "And you shall cry out on that day," he said, "because of your king whom you chose for yourself, but the Lord will not answer you on that day" (I Samuel 8:18).

The Israelite assembly rejected this Catonian warning, and chose Saul, of the tribe of Benjamin, to be their first king. Saul was a striking figure, a man among men. "There was not among the Israelites a better person than he," we are told, "from his shoulders and upward he was taller than any of the people" (I Samuel 9:2). When Samuel saw that further protest was useless, he anointed Saul, and thus the kingship over Israel was sanctified.

Trials of King Saul

Almost at once Saul's royal authority was tested; shortly after assuming office, he summoned all Israel to raise the

Ammonite siege of Jabesh-gilead in Transjordan. Saul threatened to destroy the herds of every able-bodied Israelite who failed to answer the call. He raised a force large enough to beat off the Ammonites, but the response of the tribes was still far from unanimous. Saul's close followers proposed that he destroy the slackers, but he refused. Again, in battle against the Philistines at Michmash, part of Saul's army deserted, and but for a clever strategem devised by Jonathan, the crown prince, the day would have been lost.

Then, after another victory, this time over the Amalekites, Saul's political star began to fade. The conservative element led by Samuel consistently undercut the king. Their support was grudging; they gave him little credit when he won and loudly condemned him when he lost. And meanwhile Saul was the prey of his own tempestuous and moody nature.

On one occasion Saul suddenly lost confidence in himself, when he was faced, in the Shefelah foothills near Azekah, by a Philistine army led by the giant Goliath. The once-powerful monarch was "dismayed and greatly afraid" (I Samuel 17:11). The opportunity presented itself for an unknown lad, David, son of Jesse of Bethlehem, to step into the breach. Slaying the monster Goliath, he became the boy hero of all Israel. Thereafter his rise was meteoric.

Having achieved military distinction at a very early age, David began to assume the stature of a legendary figure almost before his mature life was well begun. He is credited with having killed a lion and a bear even before his dramatic conquest of the Philistine Goliath. Because of these precocious triumphs, he won extraordinary popularity among the people.

The King Comes to Grief

Saul at first made David his protégé, married him to his daughter Michal, and acknowledged him favorite of the court. He soon realized, however, that David was becoming the center of popular favor and was threatening to reap the political rewards of fame. "Saul has slain his thousands," the people sang, "but David—his ten thousands!" Even Jonathan, the king's son, regarded David as his bosom friend. Saul tried several times to kill his younger rival. The jealous idea became fixed in Saul's head, the Biblical authors tell us (I Samuel 18–30), that if he could only rid himself of the upstart, David, all would go well with him. Finally, he drove David from the court.

David maintained his place in the hearts of the people by his gallant and resourceful acts. He sent his parents to Moab for safety, while he himself sought refuge, now at the sanctuary of Nob near Jerusalem, now at the court of Achish, the Philistine king of Gath and enemy of Saul. For a time, too, he led a band of several hundred outlaws in the Shefelah foothills in the region of Adullam. And again he proved his mettle by serving as border guard in the south for the Philistines (I Samuel 21–30). Several times during his banishment he could have killed Saul, but his deep nobility of character—and perhaps also his reverence for Saul as God's anointed one—prevented this final desperate act.

Saul died where he had first made his name, on the field of battle. Against Philistines assembled in the valley of Jezreel, Saul and his forces took up counterpositions at nearby Mount Gilboa. In the ensuing engagement the Philistines overwhelmed the Israelites, and Saul "took the

sword and fell upon it," rather than fall into the hands of
his enemies. His was a heroic and tragic role in a crucial
period in Israel's career. It was his hard lot to bear the
brunt, not only of Philistine aggression, but also of the
inevitable reaction of his own people to the decisive change
represented by his anointment as king. His sick nature,
furthermore, aggravated and dramatized the difficulties of
his position. In spite of all, however, Saul laid the foundation for an effective opposition to the Philistine advance,
for an attack on their valuable monopoly of iron, and,
perhaps most important, for a measurable degree of unifica-
tion among the individualistic tribes of Israel.

CHAPTER IV

The Israelite Empire
under David and Solomon

ANCIENT Israel's Golden Era came during the tenth century B.C., when David and Solomon ruled Israel and Israel dominated western Asia. It was this period that the prophets had in mind, later, when they urged the restoration of a united Israel and called for vengeance on the foes about them. And it was among the descendants of David that they assumed the leader would be found who could make possible this achievement. Thus Isaiah affirmed:

And there shall come forth a shoot out of the stock of Jesse [the father of David]. . . . And the spirit of the Lord shall rest upon him. . . . And it shall come to pass in that day that the root of Jesse, that stands for an ensign of the peoples, to him shall the nations seek, and his resting-place shall be glorious [11:1–10].

Recent discoveries have greatly enhanced the historical value of the Biblical account, and even enriched its three-thousand-year-old story with considerable new material. The Queen of Sheba, after she met Solomon, is reported to have exclaimed,

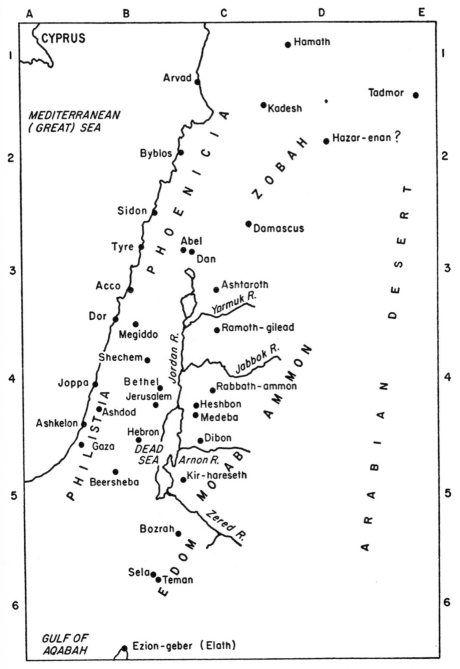

III. The united Israelite empire under David and Solomon (tenth century B.C.).

It was a true report that I heard in my country concerning your achievements and your wisdom. But I did not believe the reports until I came, and my own eyes saw. Indeed, the half of it was not told me. You have wisdom and prosperity exceeding the report that I heard [I Kings 10:6-7].

The same words might well express the mood of modern scholars rereading the Biblical history of the reigns of David and Solomon in the light of the recent revelations.

David Acquires the Throne of Saul

Left leaderless and vulnerable by their defeat at Mount Gilboa, the Israelites seemed poised on the verge of complete disintegration, like the Canaanites before them. From this fate they were saved by David and his followers.

Immediately on the death of Saul, a struggle broke out for the succession to his power. Some supported Ishbosheth (Esh-baal), a son of Saul, while others, particularly the tribe of Judah, demanded David as king (II Samuel 2-4). To seize and consolidate the royal power David had to resolve both domestic and foreign problems. On the one hand he had to acquire sole authority in Israel, and on the other hand he had to unite Israel and check the Philistine drive.

In the bloody battle which ensued, David and his followers left no room for doubt as to which group was to rule in Israel. To some supporters of Ishbosheth, death was meted out—not always, it appears, with David's knowledge or consent; to others, such as Mephibosheth, the crippled son of Jonathan, mercy was shown (II Samuel 9). Not relying completely on his fellow-Israelites, David hired mercenaries from Crete and elsewhere, the traditional

"Cherethites and Pelethites" (II Samuel 8:18; 15:18), who served as his bodyguard.

Even more important and spectacular in this swift consolidation of power and prestige were David's military triumphs. Jerusalem, also known as Jebus, the stronghold of the Jebusites, fell before his attack. Then, on several occasions, he checked the Philistines, and finally he cut them up so badly, particularly at Gath, that they never recovered their power to threaten Israel (II Samuel 21:15–22).[1] Having secured his western and southern flanks, David sent his forces east across the Jordan as far as Damascus and Zobah, and in a long series of battles he subdued some of the vigorous Aramean groups, as well as the Ammonites, Moabites, and Edomites. He even completed the destruction, which Saul had begun, of the elusive Amalekites in the south.

By the time David's astonishing military force had spent itself, the Israelites were in control of territories running from Kadesh on the Orontes River in Syria to Ezion-geber at the head of the Gulf of Aqabah. (See Map III.) The Mediterranean coast, except for Phoenicia and small segments of Philistia, had been made tributary, and Transjordan, as far as the Arabian desert on the east, also acknowledged David as king. These military triumphs, moreover, greatly furthered tribal coalescence and the composition of ancient quarrels. Already Israel was becoming a kingdom in fact, as it had been only in title under Saul.

[1] It is interesting to note that some of these battles seem to have been decided by a fight between one or more picked warriors of the two sides, as in the case of David and Goliath, or the twelve-man teams which represented the forces of David and Ishbosheth.

The Setting for International Expansion

The rise of the Israelite empire can be understood properly only in the context of the entire Near East. At the turn of the second millennium not a single state in Mesopotamia, Asia Minor, Syria, and Egypt—the aggressive forces normally active within the historic constellation of which Israel was a part—was powerful enough to interfere with David's plans for expansion. Babylonia had been in decline since the downfall of the Hammurabi dynasty in the sixteenth century B.C. The Hurrian state, in northeast Iraq, had been destroyed by Assyria in the thirteenth century. The latter, in turn (except briefly about 1100 under Tiglath-pileser I), was too weak to seek empire and adventure outside its territory until after 900 B.C. The Hittites, who had taken over northern Syria and the Hurrian state early in the fourteenth century, and whose power in the entire Near East at the time was equaled only by that of Egypt, collapsed before the onslaughts of the Aegean peoples at about 1200 B.C.

Egypt's power, too, had waned. The disintegration which had begun during the Twentieth Dynasty, especially after 1150, was not alleviated when the Amon priesthood and their wealthy associates assumed control of the land, shortly after 1100. Except for a brief period under Sheshonk I, the Biblical Shishak (about 925), Egypt was in no position to challenge anyone outside its borders until over four centuries later, when her power revived under Necho of the Twenty-sixth Dynasty. As for the Arameans (Syrians), their ascendancy in upper Transjordan, where they eventually founded a number of city-states, had only just begun.

In the context of this political void which was western Asia about 1000 B.C., the Biblical account of the rise of David's empire bears eloquent testimony to the skillful manner in which the Israelites moved to fill the vacuum.

Israel and Phoenicia

Only against Phoenicia David did not go to battle; to do so was neither necessary nor desirable. The once-great Canaanite civilization had been reduced to a narrow coastal strip running from near modern Haifa to beyond Byblos. Here the Phoenician remnant flourished.

The Israelites under David and the Phoenicians under Hiram I entered into a mutually beneficial military and political understanding. The Phoenicians agreed to provide the Israelites with skilled engineers and craftsmen, and with cedar and cypress timber from Lebanon. As a matter of fact they built David a palace (II Samuel 5:11), for which he, in turn, probably paid more in protection and non-aggression than in silver and gold. After all, Phoenicia was militarily and economically at the mercy of Israel, and it could hope to retain its independence and increase its wealth only so long as it was useful to Israel's kings.

This situation made it possible, as well as geographically necessary, for the Phoenicians to concentrate on maritime expansion. Within a very brief period they had reached almost every part of the Mediterranean basin—Spain, Sardinia, Corsica, Sicily, and north-central Africa (later Carthage)—with their commercial undertakings, colonial activity, or cultural influence. In fact, Greece and Rome (and through them ultimately a great proportion of the entire world) acquired from the Phoenicians an alphabet in which to record the *Odyssey* and the *Iliad* and the other epics which had come into being, orally perhaps, during the era corresponding to the Biblical Period of the Judges.

The New Administration

Thus within one generation the tribes of Israel came into the imperial splendor so often promised in the Pentateuch and created a national capital where none had previously existed. Shifting his headquarters from Hebron in Judah to newly conquered Jerusalem, David made this the private domain of his royal court. Existing outside all tribal jurisdiction, and belonging solely to the king, it came frequently to be called "The City of David."

The centralization of political authority in the abode of the king called for a corresponding focus for religious jurisdiction, and David's ministers began to plan the erection of a royal chapel, a magnificent edifice which would represent the earthly dwelling of Israel's invisible God. To provide fitting service for the Temple, a priesthood was established and musical guilds were organized, the latter in all likelihood by David, who was a distinguished musician and composer in his own right. Abiathar, who had assisted David at Nob, and Zadok, both of whom boasted ancient and distinguished ancestry, were appointed priests to David. Later the Zadokites, descendants real or nominal of this same Zadok, were to become the principal caste of Temple priests.

The centralization of power in David's hands was implemented further by the creation of new administrative and military systems. The boundaries of a number of tribes were altered on the excuse—plausible enough—of increasing fiscal and administrative efficiency, but more likely for the larger purpose of weakening tribal independence. The new units were to be represented at the court in Jerusalem, not in the traditional manner by the heads of the tribes and families, but by royal officials. And thus the way was paved for the collection of the taxes which were the price of monarchy.

The army was transformed into a permanent professional body, and the command reorganized to centralize control in Jerusalem directly under the king's authority. Abner, the commander-in-chief under Saul and Ishbosheth, was killed, and he was replaced by David's colorful nephew and devoted friend, Joab, one of the most underrated personalities in the Bible.

For the first time in Israelite history, the government introduced forced labor. Every able-bodied resident in Israel was made subject to labor service without compensation. This innovation, in turn, was probably the chief motivation behind the census which David caused to be taken throughout the land.

Imperial consolidation went on apace. Plans were projected for building the Temple and the government palaces in Jerusalem, and a pattern was determined for "the courses of the priests and the Levites and all the work of the service of the house of the Lord" (I Chronicles 28:11–19). David recognized the need for fortified sites scattered through the land and for administrative centers such as Megiddo. All of this involved a great building program, which, taken together with the development of the new army, the expansion of administrative services, the reorganization of the royal household, and the like, required unprecedented quantities of money, men, and supervision.

The supervision was provided by the newly created

court bureaucracy composed of scribes, heralds, recorders, ministers, stewards, and clerks, assembled in such numbers that not all of them were Israelites. To find sufficient money and manpower it was necessary to resort to booty and tribute from conquered peoples and to taxation and *corvée* at home. This vast program set the stage for David to become the great builder and organizer, as well as the military hero of Israel.

Before he could put all these magnificent plans into action, however, David died, so that his actual building was limited to the fortification of a few key sites against the Philistines, such as Tell Beit Mirsim (perhaps Biblical Kiriat-sepher) in the southern Shefelah, Beth-shemesh in the northern Shefelah, and Tell Qasileh near the Mediterranean Sea, and to the erection of royal buildings in Jerusalem and perhaps also in Megiddo.

King David, the Personality

The Biblical tradition attributes to David many qualities, but none more endearing perhaps than his gift for poetry and music. In all probability he must have composed at least some parts of the psalms which the Bible attributes to him, in addition to the famous lament over Saul and Jonathan (II Samuel 1:17–27). David's reputation was so great, however, that many psalms composed either before or after his reign came to be associated with his name. Indeed, the official collection of the first 72 psalms—though not the entire book of 150 psalms, as popular belief has since assumed—was attached to his name.

David's loves and hates have gripped the emotions and imaginations of people from his day down through the ages. Most famous of all, perhaps, was his deep affection for Jonathan, but the mere mention of David conjures up the names of Absalom, of Abigail, and the beautiful Bathsheba. In each of these stories kingly grandeur is blended with human weakness in a way that has touched and captivated each succeeding generation of readers.

On one of the rare occasions when a significant portion of the population sided with an armed revolt against David's rule, there was among the leaders David's favorite son, the charming but vacillating Absalom. Outwitted and outfought by David's well-trained militia, the rebels were defeated, although not yet crushed, when the implacable Joab brought the whole revolt to its final denouement by killing Absalom with his own hands. It was altogether characteristic of David's ofttimes unpredictable mood that he did not want any harm to come to his rebellious son and that when he heard the tragic news, "He was much moved, and went up to the chamber over the gate, and wept; and as he went, thus he said, 'O my son Absalom, my son, my son Absalom! would that I died for you, O Absalom, my son, my son!'" (II Samuel 19:1).

On those other famous occasions when he was unable to repress his passion for Abigail, whose husband he did not attempt to save from death, or for Bath-sheba, whose husband he brutally caused to be killed, David nevertheless was genuinely repentant for having caused the death of his rivals in love and humbly accepted the bitter rebuke of Nathan the prophet. It would be difficult to find another such intense, compulsive, dramatic, practical, talented personality in the wide range of human history, or so simple and powerful a delineation of character in all our literature.

To the Israelites after him, David was the key figure in the Golden Era of their history, a figure beyond reproach and beyond compare. After all, it was not he but his son and successor, Solomon, who carried out his projects to their ultimate, and frequently distasteful, conclusions. David fully deserved his place of honor in his people's history but, at the same time, it was largely a matter of good fortune that his good lived after him, whereas his evil was interred with Solomon's bones.

King Solomon

When David's end drew near, there was another contest for the royal succession, just as there had been at the death of Saul. In this characteristic the history of Israel is no different from that of any other comparable kingdoms in Assyria, Babylonia, or Egypt. The penalty for coming out second best in such a power struggle, normally, was death. So it was with Adonijah, the oldest son of David, who had prior claim over his half-brother, Solomon. Adonijah, indeed, had already been proclaimed king by his followers, including the redoubtable Joab, when Solomon's backers began a counterattack. Bath-sheba, David's favorite wife and Solomon's mother, joined with the prophet Nathan to persuade the aged king to name Solomon his legal heir. Bath-sheba pointed out that if Adonijah had his way she and her son would be as good as dead.

David let himself be swayed and gave the decisive order: "Let Zadok the priest and Nathan the prophet anoint him . . . king over Israel; and blow the trumpet, and say, 'Long live King Solomon'" (I Kings 1:34). Adonijah's followers deserted him, and Solomon later found a pretext for killing Adonijah. Other supporters of Adonijah were likewise killed or banished, until "the kingship was established firmly in the hand of Solomon" (I Kings 2:46; I Chronicles 29).

Solomon's Building Program: The Temple

Solomon inherited the task of fulfilling the plans that time and circumstances had permitted his father David only to formulate and dream about; and to this program he added plans and dreams of his own. Continuing and extending the pact with Phoenicia, Solomon imported vast amounts of timber from Lebanon and recruited large numbers of engineers, overseers, and artisans for the building of the Temple.

Solomon is best remembered by his Temple. In becoming the national shrine, as David had intended that it should, the Temple completed the process of making Jerusalem the spiritual as well as the political capital of Israel; but its cost was tremendous. To finish the magnificent edifice, Solomon was obliged to levy taxes without mercy, to force tens of thousands of his subjects to serve in labor gangs, to chop cedar and cypress in Lebanon, to raft timber from Phoenicia to Joppa, and to bear it log by log to the heights of Jerusalem.

The complex of the Temple and its associated buildings formed a magnificent architectural unit. Built by Canaanite architects, it followed the style of their native temple tradition. The two free-standing columns called Jachin and Boaz (I Kings 7:21), and the three main divisions of vestibule, holy place, and holy of holies, all sprang from the Canaanite convention. Their respective Hebrew names, *ulam*, *hekhal*, and *debir*—likewise the term *bayit* (house) for the whole Temple, which was "The House of the Lord"—also appear to have been borrowed from the Canaanites.

Solomon's regime was further distinguished by the erection of government buildings and the building or rebuilding of key fortifications. It is a frequent archaeological experience to uncover the material remains of the Solomonic (Early Iron) level of Israelite towns—for example, at Megiddo, Gezer, Tell Qasileh, Ezion-geber, Hazor, and Lachish. Like the Temple, these structures were generally Phoenician in concept and in such details as the pattern of masonry, the use of capitals (which the Greeks also borrowed from the Phoenicians a couple of centuries later), and the style of gateways.

Solomon the Merchant Prince: Ezion-geber

Of particular interest is the famous copper refinery and seaport at Ezion-geber, on the Gulf of Aqabah, rediscovered in the middle 1930's, about a third of a mile north of the present coastline. Although the site of the port had long been sought by scholars and travelers, no one was prepared for the discovery of the extraordinary structure built specifically to smelt the copper ore which was dug from the mines of nearby Sinai and Edom. Its excavator called Ezion-geber "the Pittsburgh of Palestine, in addition to being its most important port," and described Solomon "as a great copper king." Ezion-geber, like the corresponding levels from the period of Solomon at Megiddo and Tell Qasileh, "was planned in advance, and built with considerable architectural and engineering skill at one time as an integral whole." [2]

Solomon's great enterprise at Ezion-geber, with its seaport and fleet of merchant ships, would seem to clarify an intriguing Biblical problem of long standing. It has often

[2] From N. Glueck, *The Other Side of the Jordan* (New Haven, 1940), chs. iii, iv.

been asked: Did the Queen of Sheba really visit Solomon, and if so, why should she, a woman, have made the arduous and even dangerous trip of some 1,300 miles from her country in southwest Arabia to Jerusalem, bringing with her gifts of fabulous worth? The Bible explains: "Now when the Queen of Sheba heard the fame of Solomon . . . she came to test him with hard questions . . ." (I Kings 10:1–13). This explanation is clearly diplomatic. The "hard questions" very likely revolved about matters of the pocketbook. Our authority on Ezion-geber points out:

Solomon's shipping line evidently made such inroads in the lucrative caravan trade controlled by the Queen of Sheba, that she hastened to Jerusalem with all manner of presents in order to conclude an amicable trade agreement with him. . . . A satisfactory commercial treaty was evidently negotiated between the two sovereigns, because we are informed that "King Solomon gave to the Queen of Sheba all that it pleased her to ask, besides that which he gave her according to his royal bounty" [I Kings 10:13].[3]

The commercial enterprises of Solomon, handled by "the king's merchants," extended in all directions. Thus he virtually monopolized the strategic as well as lucrative horse and chariot trade; his agents bought up the horses in Cilicia and the chariots in Egypt and sold them to the Hittites, Arameans, and other peoples of the Near East (I Kings 10:28–29).

Relations with Phoenicia

The details of the economic relations between Israel and Phoenicia (cf. I Kings 5) will probably never be wholly recovered. It may be doubted that Solomon, at least in the

[3] N. Glueck, in *Biblical Archaeologist*, I (Sept., 1938), 14.

early part of his reign, paid much into Phoenicia's govern-
mental coffers for the men and materials that he received
from Hiram. After all, Phoenicia was at the mercy of Solomon no less than of David; it was not Phoenicia but Israel
which bought horses in Cilicia. On the other hand, Solomon
would have had no port, refinery, fleet, or crews at Ezion-
geber were it not for Phoenicia, and the latter did not make
this possible out of sheer good will. The Phoenicians would
have preferred to direct these projects themselves, or at least
to share in the profits, but in dealing with them Solomon
could apparently do just about as he pleased.

This relationship between Israel and Phoenicia changed
radically after the death of Solomon. Israel's united kingdom
split into two, and the military balance in the Near East
changed with the rise of Shishak in Egypt and with the
growth of the rival empires of Assyria and Aram. Phoenicia
continued to grow rich in her maritime and colonial ven-
tures and ceased to grant to Israel any more concessions or
favors.

The Administration of Solomon

Solomon perfected and extended the administrative organization initiated by his father, David (I Kings 4), and
so facilitated even more the collection of taxes and the
recruitment of forced labor. At the same time, he weakened
further the tribal loyalties.

For administrative purposes Israel was divided into twelve
districts, each with its own governor. But the areas of jurisdiction, it should be noted, did not necessarily coincide with
the old tribal territories. Excavations indicate that some of
the governors, perhaps all, lived in palaces, to which were
attached storehouses for the grain, olive oil, and cattle col-

lected as taxes in kind. Each governor was required to provide food for the royal household one month out of the year. But the district of Judah, because it provided the principal backers and lieutenants of the royal house—as well as because Jerusalem, the capital and chief city of the nation was located within its area—occupied a specially privileged position, directly under the king. At least two of the twelve governors were not only members of the tribe of Judah but sons-in-law of Solomon himself.

Culture and Religion

Writing, uncommon although far from unknown in the times of Moses and the judges, spread widely in Solomon's day. Royal secretaries recorded the affairs of state, and royal archives are referred to repeatedly in the books of Kings and Chronicles, with some variation of the formula: "And the rest of the acts of King So-and-So and all that he did, behold they are inscribed in the records of the royal chronicles of Israel and Judah." Unfortunately, however, these records have not yet been recovered by excavators.

The royal annals, in keeping with the classical Hebrew narrative style of such other books as Judges and Samuel, were written in a highly developed Hebrew prose. Israel's poets, moreover, stood on the same high level as her writers of prose, as can readily be seen from the few samples that have been preserved, for example: Moses' Song of Triumph at the Red Sea (Exodus 15, in part), the Blessing of Moses (Deuteronomy 33, in part), the Oracles of Balaam (Numbers 23–24), and the Song of Deborah (Judges 5).

The books of the Pentateuch began to take shape from material that for centuries had been orally transmitted from generation to generation. Solomon himself was a patron

of literature and the arts, and it is not accidental that his
name became intimately associated with such classics as
Proverbs, Canticles, and Ecclesiastes even though these
books crystallized in their present written form after the
Babylonian Exile.

It was, however, during Solomon's reign that a tendency
toward toleration and assimilation of alien religious ideas
first increased to prominence. Canaanite elements were responsible for the main divergences from the worship of
the Lord. Economic and political co-operation between
Israel and Phoenicia led to the free exchange of cultural
and religious practices as well. The worship of Baal and
other prominent Phoenician deities, including some of their
orgiastic elements, spread in Israel. Intermarriage with Phoenician and other non-Israelite peoples also became less rare.
The king himself "loved many foreign women, besides the
daughter of Pharaoh, women of the Moabites, Ammonites,
Edomites, Sidonians, and Hittites" (I Kings 11:1 ff.). It is
true that Solomon's acquisition of many of the alleged total
of "seven hundred princesses and three hundred concu-
bines" was motivated, as royal marriages frequently are, by
the dictates of diplomacy. But these casual marriages with
foreigners brought in their wake additional concessions to
alien gods. The Biblical writers did not overlook the fact
that Solomon built idolatrous shrines for Ashtoreth, Mil-
com, Chemosh, Molech, Asherah, and other deities of the
foreign princesses, just as he permitted Phoenician novelties
to intrude among various aspects of the Temple cult and
paraphernalia.

Tens of thousands of Israelites of the border regions of
Dan, Asher, Zebulun, Naphtali, and Manasseh mingled bus-
ily with the Phoenicians. Also in commercial towns such as

Tell Qasileh and border towns such as Beth-shemesh, Israelites and non-Israelites freely mixed. Small wonder that the Biblical historians of the Book of Kings blamed Solomon for this apostasy from the Lord, which, in their opinion, accounted largely for the disruption of the kingdom and the other disasters which followed his death (I Kings 11:9–13).

The Last Days of the United Kingdom

The opulence and power of Solomon's kingdom was doomed to deteriorate. Under the increasing pressure of this decline, tensions, both foreign and domestic, produced a split between politically favored Judah in the south and the northern districts which came to call themselves Israel —with "Israel" here representing a political and not a spiritual unit.

In Israel as well as Judah, Solomon's rule brought great prosperity and prestige to the land, but it was only in a limited degree that the common people shared with the aristocracy in this new wealth and status. Forced labor, high taxes, and political corruption bred a host of enemies for the king's regime.

These grievances further aggravated the ancient distrust and resentment of the northern tribes for the Judeans and their assumed superiority. Even before Solomon's reign had drawn to its close, the situation had become critical. When Rehoboam, Solomon's son and successor, sent his tax collector, Adoniram, to treat with the Israelites under Jeroboam, he was confronted with open revolt. Adoniram was stoned to death, and Rehoboam himself barely escaped with his life (I Kings 12; II Chronicles 10). This act of violence ushered in the Divided Kingdom.

The rebel leaders of northern Israel did not oppose a

monarchy, nor did they care about the kind of worship that went on in the Temple and the shrines. They were willing to support one of their own as king, in the hope and belief that this would lighten the heavy burden of taxation and increase their share in the common wealth. But the lower classes who made up the backbone of the rebellion in the North had yet to learn that what Jeroboam and the other northern leaders intended was nothing more than replacing the Judean monarchy of Solomon with another equally harsh monarchy of their own.

The Biblical historian makes it clear that if the ruling group behind Rehoboam had been willing to share the considerable wealth of the kingdom with the leading supporters of Jeroboam, the kingdom of Solomon would have endured (I Kings 12:1-19). Whether there simply was not enough wealth to satisfy both groups, or whether Rehoboam overestimated his strength, the fact remains that the North broke forever with the South.

CHAPTER V

The Divided Kingdom: Israel and Judah

ISRAELITE civilization was not destined to make any important contributions to mankind's material progress. The physical and economic geography of the land constituted a formidable obstacle to any such achievement. The natural resources of the region lying between Dan and Beersheba were few, its population small, and economic surpluses, therefore, negligible. Unlike the Egyptians, Phoenicians, and such peoples of western Asia as the Sumerians, Babylonians, and Assyrians, the Israelites never won a major place among the great builders, merchants, or warriors of the ancient Near East.

Israel's defensive situation was not more fortunate. Having made their home in a buffer area amid stronger civilizations, the Israelites were under almost constant pressure or attack from neighbors striving, if not to conquer them outright, at least to use their land as a highway or base for invasion of some rival. Once David's reign was over, the momentary lull in the imperial struggles of western Asia came to an end. Without such a lull the Israelite empire could hardly have emerged at all; and when it was over,

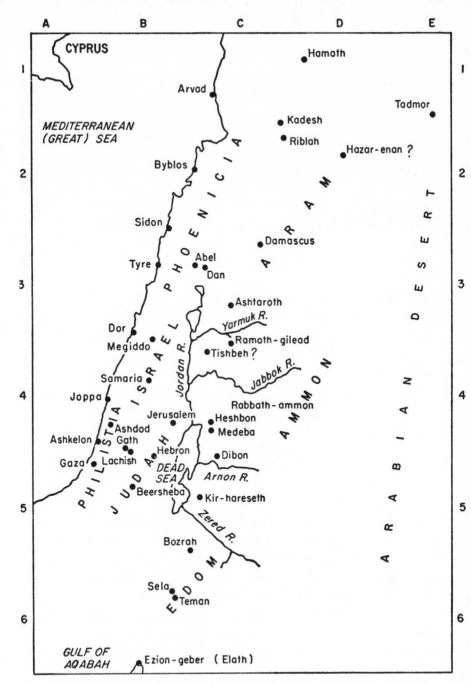

IV. The Divided Kingdom: Israel and Judah (ninth and eighth centuries B.C.).

Judah and Israel had no rest. Actual invasions were not uncommon, and the threat of possible or impending attack was almost constant. These same conditions, on the other hand, provided the setting for the Israelite genius which came to express itself in the realm of culture and religion; and it was largely during the period of the Divided Kingdom that the Israelite civilization took on its definite shape and character.

The split between Judah and Israel, following the revolt of Jeroboam, leader of the northern rebels, against Rehoboam, successor to Solomon, resulted in a stalemate. Israel, the northern segment, being larger both in total arable land and population, was wealthier than its rival. But if Judah, from whose soil the state of David had sprung, was smaller and geographiclly more concentrated, it was for that reason more efficiently administered and far less torn by regional conflicts. Israel was united chiefly by its opposition to Judah.

Had the two kingdoms been left to themselves, either might have gained the ascendancy over its opponent. But the major factors in preserving an equilibrium were external. Egypt, for a short time, and then Aram and Assyria managed to preserve a balance of power between the two.

The International Setting: Egypt, Aram, Assyria

After lying dormant several centuries, Egypt began to show renewed signs of imperial vigor under Shishak, founder of the Twenty-second Dynasty. By harboring such enemies of Solomon as Jeroboam and Hadad the Edomite, Shishak had helped to prepare the split of united Israel and then, exploiting the break which followed Solomon's death, he moved at once to invade the southern kingdom of Judah.

Anticipating an Egyptian invasion, Rehoboam shelved

the idea of challenging the secessionist government of Israel and instead made a feverish attempt to strengthen his own defenses (II Chronicles 11:5–12). These efforts proved of no avail when Shishak's army began to march (about 920 B.C.): the fortified cities of Judah fell one after another, and the treasures of the palace and Temple in Jerusalem fell into the enemy's hands.

At first, northern Israel welcomed the breathing spell provided by Egypt's invasion of Judah. But Shishak's mixed hordes did not stop at the boundaries of Judah; they pushed on into the territory of Israel, as well as south into Edom and west into Philistia. Difficulties at home, however, prevented Shishak from exploiting this brilliant beginning; yet in one respect, at least, this isolated imperialist irruption was of great significance: it left Judah unable to re-establish its old predominance over Israel.

The split between Israel and Judah considerably facilitated the emergence of several Aramean states in the northern part of the area that lay between Israel and the Euphrates, i.e., Syria. The powerful state of David and Solomon had held this area in check; but divided, Israel and Judah were less successful. Now and then they joined forces against the Arameans, and at other times one or the other entered into a coalition with an Aramean state against her sister state.

Even Phoenicia failed to maintain its independence. Faced by the growing power first of the Arameans and later of the Assyrians, the Phoenicians continued to cultivate their neighborly relations with Israel. This policy led, among other things, to the marriage of Ahab, son of King Omri of Israel, to Jezebel, daughter of King Ittobaal of Phoenicia. But early in the ninth century, the Assyrian Ashurnasirpal

II (about 883–859) managed to reduce parts of Phoenicia to tributary status and at the same time to establish the reputation of the Assyrian armies for merciless brutality.

The Assyrian menace provoked a reaction in the form of a defensive coalition in the region headed by the Israelites and Arameans. The royal Assyrian chronicle recounts that King Ahab of Israel contributed 2,000 chariots and 10,000 foot soldiers to the coalition; but, in spite of this magnificence, its forces were defeated at the battle of Karkar, near Hamath (about 853). It does not appear that the Assyrians were able to exploit the victory at once; but within ten years they were collecting tribute from states as far west as Israel and Phoenicia. From then until the Medes and a resurgent Babylonia brought her to heel some two and a half centuries later, Assyria held all of western Asia in her sway. The history of Judah and Israel must be read against this background.

The Northern Kingdom of Israel

From the breakup of Solomon's kingdom no single major group ever managed to dominate Israel for more than a generation or two at a time. Chronic plotting for the succession repeatedly brought kings and would-be kings to bloody ends, until after years of civil war a military chieftain named Omri finally gained the upper hand (about 878) and established what the Assyrian royal chronicles called the "House of Omri" (I Kings 15:9 ff.; 16:1–23).

The Omride Dynasty

It was under Omri that the northern kingdom acquired, for the first time, a permanent and impressive capital. Abandoning Tirzah, which had served as a kind of capital for about forty years, Omri built a new political center, which he named Samaria. From the excavations at this site, a good picture is gained of the magnificent palace and fortifications which he and his son Ahab erected there. And recent excavation has assigned to their period the mammoth stables erected at Megiddo; they housed many of the horses harnessed to Ahab's 2,000 chariots employed at Karkar.

The house of Omri brought prosperity to the northern kingdom. Aram for the time being ceased to threaten, Moab in Transjordan was under control, and economic relations with Phoenicia developed rapidly. This prosperity, however, was restricted almost exclusively to Israel's upper class. Those who worked with their hands in the towns and on the land shared little enough in this new wealth. The petty farmer frequently lost his crops and his land to the big landowner. The apprentices and artisans found the economic and social gap widening between themselves and their masters. The merchant class became richer and more influential than before. Freemen were becoming slaves, and the poor were being compelled to sell their children into bondage. Where members of the lower classes were able to obtain loans from the rich, it was usually at exorbitant rates of interest. Nor was the economic and social structure helped by the periodic droughts which came upon the land, such as the drought and famine recorded in the days of Ahab.

Ahab, Naboth, and Elijah

During this period occurred that event recorded in I Kings 21 and celebrated in the annals of justice and literature. Naboth, a commoner, owned a vineyard next to Ahab's palace. The king, determined to acquire the land, made several offers; but Naboth, a man of strong ancestral sentiment, would not sell the property he had inherited from his fathers. Thereupon Jezebel, Ahab's Phoenician wife, bribed two men to accuse Naboth falsely of blasphemy and treason. Naboth and his heirs were stoned to death, and the vineyard fell to the king.

The injustice of the royal couple was bluntly denounced by the prophet Elijah. "Have you murdered, and you will take possession too?" And he went on to curse the king, saying, "So said the Lord, 'In the place where the dogs licked the blood of Naboth, the dogs shall lick your own blood'" (I Kings 21:19).

In denouncing the attempt of the monarchy to nullify the property and other rights of the old order, Elijah was acting in the same tradition as the prophet Nathan in the previous century, who fearlessly condemned David for causing the death of Uriah, the husband of Bath-sheba (II Samuel 11–12).

The Dynasty of Jehu

A revolt against the son of Ahab (about 842) brought Jehu to the throne. The new monarch initiated a sweeping purge of the Omride household and its chief supporters. He killed Jezebel and all of Ahab's heirs and "all who remained of the house of Ahab in Jezreel" (II Kings 10:11).

When King Hazael of Aram threatened Israel, Jehu paid tribute to Shalmaneser of Assyria to keep the Syrian ruler in check. This event has become famous because Shalmaneser's Black Obelisk, discovered in his palace in 1846, records and illustrates the transaction. The bas-relief clearly pictures the Israelite delegation, headed by a prostrate figure

—either Jehu or his personal deputy—bringing the tribute to "the mighty monarch."

Later, when the Assyrians developed troubles of their own at home, their domination of Israel was replaced by that of the Arameans, under Hazael and his son Ben-hadad. But Aram, in its turn, was rent and weakened by civil war, thus giving the kingdom of Israel the opportunity to embark once again on an expanded period of expansion and prosperity.

The long reign of Jeroboam II witnessed the spectacular, if temporary, reconquest of a considerable part of the area originally controlled by David and Solomon. The territory across the Jordan which had been lost to Aram was recovered. The Bible records that Jeroboam "restored the boundary of Israel from the entrance of Hamath as far as the Sea of the Arabah" (II Kings 14:25). None of Assyria, Aram, or Judah was in a position to interfere with Israel's limited objectives, and the Phoenicians profited with Israel through their long-established policy of co-operation. Excavations of such cities as Samaria and Megiddo have uncovered striking evidence of Israel's increased wealth during this period. It seemed that northern Israel was again well on the way to prosperity and peace.

Amos and Hosea

Once more, however, royal arrogance and privilege provoked a ringing challenge. As Nathan had confronted David, as Elijah had rebuked Ahab and Jezebel, now Amos spoke out, even at the temple of Bethel in Israel. From his position as a herdsman of Tekoa in Judah, Amos saw in the life of his people a gloomy picture within the gilded frame of royal riches. As fast as the upper classes were acquiring wealth, the poorer groups were sinking into a disastrous economic decline. He realized that in such social quicksand Israel could not endure.

In tirades which have never been equaled in their majestic force or terrible beauty, Amos denounced King Jeroboam II. Like Elijah and Elisha before him, like Deborah, Samuel, and Nathan before them, Amos saw in his God the complete sovereign not only of His own chosen land and people but of the peoples and lands which surrounded Israel as well. The king and his supporters, Amos warned, had broken the Covenant with God: "They sold the righteous for money, and the needy for the price of a pair of sandals." In the name of God, Amos portrayed with thunderous phrase the mortal peril of a society in which the powerful "trample the head of the poor into the dust of the earth, and turn aside the way of the humble . . . so that they have profaned My holy name" (Amos 2:6–7).

The same dire warning was hurled at Israel by the prophet Hosea, an Israelite contemporary of Amos. Knowing intimately all phases of her life, Hosea dwelt upon Israel's faithless desertion of the Lord for the gods of the Phoenicians and the idols of the heathen. Her leaders and priests, even her prophets, he charged, shared in the common acts of sin and sacrilege. Thus to depend on fortified cities, on impotent idols, and on Assyrian might, he warned Israel, was to invite disaster and exile. Only if Israel turned back to God, could the catastrophe be averted:

> Samaria shall bear her guilt,
>   Because she had rebelled against her God.
> They shall fall by the sword,
>   Their infants shall be dashed in pieces,
>   And their pregnant women ripped open.

> Return, O Israel, to the Lord your God,
> For you have stumbled in your iniquity
> [Hosea 14:1-2; 13:16 f. in English versions].

The warnings of Amos and Hosea were fulfilled. The dynasty of Jehu, like that of Omri, came to a catastrophic end about 750.

The Fall of Israel

By this time, in truth, it made very little difference who ruled Israel, for Assyria once again had begun its massive westward thrust in the greatest phase of its imperialist expansion. Tiglath-pileser III conquered all of western Asia and carried off to distant lands large segments of the conquered populations.

Menahem, the reigning King of Israel, prevented the total devastation of the country only by paying heavy tribute, which he raised with a crushing levy on the people.

The new Israelite administration, however, not being content to remain a mere vassal of Assyria, withheld tribute on several occasions and began negotiations for a coalition with Egypt. Thus flouted, the Assyrians decided to put a stop, once and for all, to the spirit of resistance and intrigue which still smoldered in Israel. The Assyrian army under Shalmaneser V marched into Israel and for three years besieged the capital Samaria. Not until Shalmaneser was succeeded by his commander-in-chief, Sargon II, did the Assyrians smash through the crumbling defenses and put the city to fire and sword. Thus the sovereignty of the northern kindom of Israel came to a final end (about 722).

Sargon always took great pride in his capture of Samaria. He records in his Annals that he led away as booty 27,290 of its inhabitants. The resulting depletion of Israel by forced exile had its counterpart in the resettlement throughout the land of Canaan of Babylonians, Elamites, Arameans, and others drawn from other conquered territories. This deportation has given rise to a double misconception: first, that there were ten tribes in northern Israel at the time of its destruction, and secondly, that these ten tribes were "lost," only to reappear elsewhere in the world. Time and again, peoples the world over have claimed descent from these "Ten Lost Tribes."

There were not, in fact, ten distinct tribes in Israel at the time of Sargon the Assyrian; and the exiles were lost only in the sense that they were absorbed wherever they were transplanted. Probably only a few of the descendants of the Israelite exiles remained true to the God and land of Israel and managed, nearly a century and a half later, to join with the exiles of Judah.

The foreigners who were thus introduced into Israel also tended to lose their cultural identity in a general amalgamation. It was this resettlement, with its inevitable effect on religious and social customs, which set the stage for the rise of the anti-Judean group among the Samaritans that resisted the restoration of Jerusalem and the Temple later on when the Persians had come to power.

The Southern Kingdom of Judah

The history of Judah generally paralleled that of Israel, with the one qualification that Judah tended to be weak when Israel was strong. The area from Dan to Beersheba, with its limited natural resources and economic advantages, did not seem able to support two prosperous kingdoms at once. Agriculture, commerce, the handicrafts, and the tribute of weaker nations formed the major sources of income of both countries. Further, the intervention of neighboring powers—whether Assyria, the Aramean states, Phoenicia,

Egypt, or the Transjordan countries—tended to keep the two divided and unequal. Only occasionally did circumstances combine to allow an effective and equal alliance between Israel and Judah.

In spite of its inherent weakness, however, Judah lasted longer. Consisting of only two tribes, Judah and Benjamin, both of which remained loyal to the line and tradition of David, it was more compact and capable of greater coherence and agility. Nor did it lie directly across the path of conquerors.

During most of the long reigns of Asa and his son Jehoshaphat (about 912–850), Judah and the dynasty of David continued to prosper. Asa's administration stabilized the position of the land. Asa checked the Egyptian army under Zerah the Ethiopian at Mareshah (II Chronicles 14:8–14) and bribed Ben-hadad of Aram to attack Baasha of Israel, to force the king to raise his siege of northern Judah.

Asa also carried out a program of religious reform. Early in his career he abolished male prostitution and various forms of idolatry, alien elements which had no rightful place alongside the worship of the Lord. In all of this he had the vigorous encouragement of the prophet Azariah.

Faced by the growing menace of the Arameans and Assyrians, Jehoshaphat then concluded a pact with Israel, and his son Joram (or Jehoram) was married to Athaliah, daughter (or sister) of Ahab. But not all the Judeans favored the alliance of the government with that of Ahab. Indeed, on one occasion when Jehoshaphat returned from an ill-starred joint military venture with Israel against Ramoth-gilead in Transjordan, then in Aramean hands, Jehu, son of Hanani the seer denounced him: "Should you help the wicked, and love those who hate the Lord?" (I Kings 22; II Chronicles 18; 19:2).

The Judean government levied tribute on the Philistines and Arabs, garrisoned the fortified cities of the land, and defeated a coalition of Ammonites, Moabites, and Edomites. For a time Judah held sway over the southern part of Transjordan all the way to Ezion-geber. Jehoshaphat rebuilt the harbor there and in a joint venture with Ahab's older son Ahaziah launched a new merchant fleet. The prophet Eliezer protested vehemently against this act of co-operation with Israel (II Chronicles 20:25-27; I Kings 22:48-49). In any case, the ships were wrecked, and the project was not repeated. But in another joint venture with Israel, that of collecting tribute from the Moabites, Jehoshaphat was somewhat more successful.

Judicial Reforms

An important development in this period was the reorganization of the Judean judicial system. The authority of the "elders" and the "heads of the tribes" had been on the wane ever since the days of the United Kingdom. The Bible reports that David and Solomon themselves acted as judges (II Samuel 15:2-6; I Kings 3:9-12) and appointed judges who, like the district governors, were responsible directly to them. Even the priests and Levites who administered the religious law and formed a kind of civil service were personally responsible to the king.

Probably because the civil administration of justice had become corrupt (II Chronicles 19:6-7) Jehoshaphat cleaned out the old system and appointed Levites, priests, and prominent laymen to administer both the religious and civil law. The Bible says of this reform:

And, behold, Amariah the chief priest shall be over you in all [religious] matters of the Lord, and Zebadiah the son of Ishmael, the leader of the house of Judah, shall be over you in all

the king's [civil] matters; and the officers of the Levites shall
be before you. Deal courageously, and may the Lord be with
the good! [II Chronicles 19:11].

In all likelihood, the religious and civil spheres of the law
were frequently too closely intertwined to be administered
separately by religious and lay officials. In any case, it would
appear that the judicial reforms of Jehoshaphat made it
easier for the high priest to replace the king as the chief
judge of the land after the return from the Babylonian Exile.

Conflict and Respite

During the reign of Jehoshaphat's son, Joram (or Jehoram), and the brief reigns of his successors, Judah's position
deteriorated steadily, allowing the Edomites to revolt and
achieve a measure of independence. During this period
Philistine and Arabian marauders even invaded the royal
palace and made off with its treasures, the royal wives, and
all the princes but one.

Ahaziah, the lone survivor, reigned but one year; and
following his death, his mother Athaliah proceeded to mur-
der all but one of her grandsons and usurp the throne. Thus
a full-blooded Phoenician woman, Jezebel, was the power
behind the throne of Ahab in Israel, and her half-Phoenician
daughter was on the throne in Judah. Six years later, Athaliah
was killed and Joash (or Jehoash), the single grandson who
had escaped her murderous net, assumed the kingship about
836. Under Joash and his son Amaziah, Judah's troubles
continued.

Finally, during the long reign of his grandson Uzziah
(II Kings 14; II Chronicles 25) and the latter's son and
coregent Jotham (about 775–735), Judah reached the peak

of its power and prosperity. Free of any threat of interference by Israel, Uzziah was able to effect impressive improvements in his people's position both at home and abroad. The army was enlarged, reorganized, and supplied with the latest weapons and engines of siege. Key sites were fortified. Recalcitrant Philistine cities were reduced to subjection. The peoples of Transjordan were conquered and laid under tribute. In the Negeb, all the way to Ezion-geber and even beyond into Arabia, agriculture, commerce, and building flourished as never before (II Chronicles 26).

With the accession of Tiglath-pileser III to the throne of Assyria, Judah felt the need of a defensive coalition with Israel, Aram, and other nations against the revived Mesopotamian menace. Yet it was with the greatest difficulty that the little kingdom, now ruled by Jotham's son Ahaz, retained some semblance of her former independence. On one occasion Ahaz purchased Tiglath-pileser's assistance in driving off the allied armies of Aram and Israel (about 735); and just over a decade later Ahaz had to repeat this act of submission, during Israel's fatal revolt against Assyria.

Judah's tribute to Assyria must have been considerable, yet on the surface her prosperity appeared to continue. This impression may have been due, in part at least, to the fact that her surrounding rivals had likewise been weakened by Assyria.

Under Hezekiah and Manasseh: Micah

After Israel's fall, Merodach-baladan, king of Babylon, tried to form a coalition with Judah and organize western Asia to defy Assyria. Isaiah came forth and warned Hezekiah, son of Ahaz, that Judah would be trapped in the middle of a bitter struggle. The prophet thundered:

Hear the word of the Lord. Behold, the days are coming when all that is in your house, and that which your fathers treasured up until this day, will be carried off to Babylon. . . . And some of your sons who are born to you shall be taken captive, and they shall be eunuchs in the palace of the king of Babylon [II Kings 20:16–18; Isaiah 39:6–7].

Isaiah was joined by another prophet, Micah, native of Moresheth, near Philistine Gath in the Shefelah. In the spirit of Hosea before him, who had described Israel as "mixing herself among the nations . . . like a silly dove, without understanding" (Hosea 7:8–11), Micah had already excoriated Israel for her reliance on the power of foreign allies instead of on the strength of the Lord. Now in His name he warned the people again:

> I will make of Samaria heaps in the field,
>   A place for planting vineyards,
> And I will pour down her stones into the valley,
>   And her foundations I will uncover [Micah 1:6].

Moreover, he continued, Israel's doom would extend to Judah, for Judah was guilty of the same sins:

> The godly man has perished from the land,
>   And the upright among men is no more.
> They all lie in wait for blood,
>   And each stalks his brother with a net [Micah 7:2]

Judah's leaders, her prophets, her judges, her priests, and her rich men were all misleading her. Trusting only in burnt offerings and empty sacrifices, they ignored Micah's classic injunction:

> Only to do justice
>   and to love loyally
>   and to walk humbly with your God [6:8].

The ominous warnings of Isaiah and Micah went un-
heeded. Shortly after 715, Assyria invaded the rebellious
states and crushed them. Another major invasion took place
about 701. The Assyrian forces under Sennacherib sub-
jugated most of western Asia, and the enemy threatened
Jerusalem itself. Interestingly, the Biblical account of this
event (II Kings 18-19; Isaiah 36-38) is supplemented by the
Assyrian chronicle. Together they paint a vivid picture of
the campaign. Sennacherib, in his chronicle, boasts:

As for Hezekiah the Judean, he did not submit to my yoke, I
laid siege to 46 of his strong cities, walled forts, and to the
countless small villages in their vicinity, and conquered them.
. . . I drove out of them 200,150 people. . . . [Hezekiah]
himself I made a prisoner in Jerusalem, his royal residence, like
a bird in a cage.[1]

The Assyrian army, however, did not take Jerusalem.
A plague, achieving what the Judeans could not, laid the
invaders low and spared the city. As the story is told by
the Biblical chronicler:

That night the angel of the Lord went forth and struck 185,-
000 in the camp of Assyria. And when men arose early in the
morning, behold, they were all dead corpses. And Sennacherib
king of Assyria departed, and went and returned, and dwelt
at Nineveh [II Kings 19:35-36].

During the reign of Hezekiah, several religious reforms
were effected (II Chronicles 29-30). The Temple and its
paraphernalia were purified, the priestly and Levitic orders
were reorganized, idolatrous objects and sites throughout
the land were destroyed, and the celebration of the passover, long neglected by many, was once more generally

[1] After A. Leo Oppenheim, in *Ancient Near Eastern Texts*, ed.
J. B. Pritchard (Princeton, 1950), p. 288.

revived. But the long reign of Hezekiah's son, Manasseh, traditionally fifty-five years and the longest in the history of Judah or Israel, was remembered by the Biblical writer for "the evil that he did in the eyes of the Lord" (II Kings 21:2). He reintroduced the idolatrous objects and shrines which his father had removed, and "shed . . . much innocent blood, until he had filled Jerusalem from one end to another." But it must be borne in mind that during this period Judah was a vassal of the Assyrians (about 680–635).

Josiah and the Reformation: Jeremiah

King Josiah, Manasseh's grandson, possibly with the full knowledge of Assyria, began to act with a remarkable show of independence; he seems even to have entertained hopes of taking over Israel, now an Assyrian colony. The Judean government was able to reorganize and enlarge the army, as well as to nurture other bold designs, because Assyria was being challenged by powerful peoples round about her in Mesopotamia.

About 621, while catastrophe was brewing for Assyria and, unbeknown to anyone, for Judah as well, Josiah effected the sweeping religious reforms subsequently known as the Reformation of Josiah. Unlike so many of his predecessors, Josiah was not content merely to cleanse the Temple of idolatrous objects and rites and to reorganize its services and priesthood. Rounding up the priests who had abetted alien practices, Josiah had them slain, and at the same time he abolished all shrines except the Temple in Jerusalem. He incorporated the dislodged priests in the purged guild at Jerusalem (II Kings 22–23).

The religious occasion for this reform was the accidental discovery, during a rebuilding of the Temple, of the Book of the Law (or Covenant). This document, found by the high priest Hilkiah, had evidently been pigeonholed and forgotten during some earlier "wicked" regime. Hilkiah's scroll is now generally supposed to have contained a basic part of the book of Deuteronomy.

It was in fact at about this time that the Book of Deuteronomy seems to have taken on the form we know today. The method employed by the editor apparently was to take the older traditions, the bare bones of the Mosaic experience, the themes of national covenant and chosen people, and amplify them in terms of the prophetic tradition. The purpose was to drive home the idea that all Israel was a community bound and locked to a God who would reward those who obeyed Him and punish those who did not.

Jeremiah the prophet had supported and encouraged Josiah's reformation. But the reforms do not appear to have affected the Judean population deeply nor to have lasted long. Jeremiah found it necessary to dissociate himself from the project and to lament its deterioration.

In the last years of Josiah's reign, the Assyrian empire began to crumble; by 612 the Babylonians, Medes, and Scythians had destroyed it forever and leveled its capital, the fabled Nineveh, in the dust. This shattering event was taken by the prophet Nahum as his theme to demonstrate the retributive justice of the God of Israel. Beginning with the traditional avowal:

> The Lord is a jealous and avenging God,
>   The Lord avenges and is full of wrath;
> The Lord takes vengeance on His adversaries,
>   And He reserves wrath for His enemies. . . .

he ends his Oracle concerning Nineveh with a somber, almost elegiac, triumph:

Your shepherds are asleep, O king of Assyria,
Your nobles slumber;
Your people are scattered on the mountains,
And there is none to gather them. . . .

Near Eastern Ferment and the Fall of Judah

Assyria's fall only paved the way for new and greater disasters. The Egyptians, reviving under Necho, rushed into the vacuum left by the Assyians and made an effort to gain control of western Asia. Fearful of this threat, Josiah moved north into the valley of Jezreel to intercept the Egyptian advance. He took his stand at strategic Megiddo (609), but his Judean forces were overwhelmed and Josiah himself was killed (II Kings 23:29).

His son Jehoahaz II (Shallum) succeeded to the throne; but three months later Necho dragged him off in chains to the Nile and replaced him with Jehoiakim (Eliakim), another of Josiah's sons. In the meantime, however, Babylonia, the most rapidly growing power in Mesopotamia, inflicted a crushing defeat on Necho's forces at Carchemish (605) and succeeded the Assyrians as overlords of western Asia.

For a time, Jehoiakim vacillated, now looking hopefully to Babylonia, now to his Egyptian sponsors. Judah did not yet realize that Egypt would never recover from the catastrophe at Carchemish and would itself become but a dependency of other powers. Forgotten was the ancient warning: "Behold, you are putting your trust on the staff of this bruised reed, on Egypt, upon which if anyone lean, it will go into the hand and pierce it. So is Pharaoh, king of Egypt, to all who put their trust in him" (II Kings 18:21; Isaiah 36:6).

This indecision was rudely resolved when Babylonia,

under the energetic leadership of the ascendant Chaldean minority headed by Nebuchadnezzar, dispatched an army that swiftly subdued all of Judah. Even then, however, Nebuchadnezzar had no sooner turned his back than Jehoiakim revolted in a desperate gamble on aid from Egypt. But even as Jeremiah had warned, this aid never came. The Chaldean conqueror replied by sending a punitive force back into Judah, and the enemy captured Jerusalem, though only after strenuous resistance.

About three months before this Babylonian expedition actually breached the city, Jehoiakim was slain, apparently the victim of a palace plot. It was his young son Jehoiachin (Jeconiah), successor on the throne, who caught the full weight of the Babylonian vengeance. He and all the royal household, together with a portion of the upper class and a great levy of craftsmen, were marched off as captives to Babylon. As puppet ruler, the conqueror left on the throne Mattaniah, a son of Josiah, and changed his name to Zedekiah (II Kings 24:17; I Chronicles 3:15).

After some ten years of Babylonian rule, Judah revolted a second time, again refusing to heed Jeremiah's dismal warnings to rely on the Lord and not on the force of arms. This time Babylonia struck back with even greater fury, not merely to bring the rebellious province to the dust, but to dispel any dreams of like resurgence on the part of Egypt.

The Babylonians systematically took and razed all the fortified cities of Judah. Archaeological excavation has confirmed the thoroughness of this destruction. Jerusalem, the capital, held out for almost two years, but fierce hunger and the Babylonian siege engines finally broke through the defenses and forced capitulation (586). The conquerors leveled the Temple to the ground. "They captured the king, and brought him up to the king of Babylonia to Riblah [near Kadesh], and judgment was passed on him. They slew the sons of Zedekiah before his eyes, and put out the eyes of Zedekiah, and bound him in fetters, and took him to Babylon" (II Kings 25:6–7). There followed renewed deportations of the people from their land. The sovereign state of Judah was no more.

Now the Babylonians reduced Judah to the status of an outright colony, similar to that endured by Israel since the days of the Assyrian rule. A native Judean, Gedaliah by name, was appointed governor of the despoiled and depopulated land and established headquarters at Mizpah. Gedaliah's administration seems to have been mild, for many Judeans who had fled into the hills, or into Egypt or Transjordan, returned from their places of refuge. But a certain Ishmael, a member of the Judean royal house, was desirous of restoring the monarchy and, abetted by the Ammonites, conspired to throw off Babylon's yoke. His well-meaning but utterly irresponsible accomplices murdered Gedaliah, together with the Judeans and Babylonians who made up his retinue, and embarked upon a reign of terror in the land. Once again the revenge of Babylon was swift and terrible. In 582 her troops instituted the third and final phase of Judah's depopulation and destruction (II Kings 25; Jeremiah 41–42).

Finally peace was achieved. Judah lay quiet, all the swirl and clash of centuries apparently come to naught. The period of the Great Babylonian Exile descended upon the people of Judah, God's people. But the Law remained, and all that it stood for and implied.

CHAPTER VI

The Babylonian Exile
and the Restoration of Judah

THE Babylonian Exile was a supreme test of Israel's vitality. The Judeans were the only people in ancient times known to have been taken wholesale into captivity and still to have retained their religious and social identity. The Exile proved that Israel—the spiritual community—could adapt itself to, and develop under, the most adverse conditions. In fact, the very adversity seems to have bred leaders whose religious experience climaxed the prophetic tradition. Many Judeans lost faith in God. According to the Covenant He was their infallible protector; but in the contest with the Babylonian gods, He obviously had been worsted. There were others, however, who believed, also on covenantal grounds, that the Lord had visited destruction on Judah as a punishment for its wickedness; and it was this idea which was championed by the prophetic movement.

The Exile, in addition, marked the beginning of a slow transition of Judaism to a form which was destined to evolve during the period of the Second Commonwealth and set the pattern for Jewish life during the Diaspora, or great dispersion, which took place after the Romans destroyed Jerusalem in 70 A.D.

Devastation in Judah

The land of Judah, itself, lay for a time inert, physically reduced, its remnants of population bereft of direction and spirit. Recent excavations at such sites as Lachish, Bethshemesh, and Tell Beit Mirsim (perhaps Kiriat-sepher) bear eloquent testimony to the devastation wreaked on the rebellious kingdom of Judah by the forces of Chaldea. In 1935 a number of *ostraca*—potsherds used as writing material—were dug up at Lachish. Most of these appear to have been military dispatches written about 587 B.C. and record a determined struggle on the part of the Judean garrisons against the more powerful Babylonian enemy. The writer of Ostracon VI expressed deep concern about rumors of defeatism among the ruling class in Jerusalem: "And behold the words of the (princes) are not good, but to weaken our hands." Significantly, these relics were found buried deep in ashes.

Many towns in Judah were so thoroughly leveled by the Babylonians that they never were restored. The Temple, and the central religious organization too, was totally destroyed. The normal leaders of the community—the well to do, the well educated, even the artisans—were either carried off to Babylon or fled to Transjordan and Egypt. Indeed, when Gedaliah was murdered, Jeremiah urged his fellow Judeans to remain in the land; but a group took Jeremiah forcibly with them into Egypt (Jeremiah 41–43).

As the Judean social order thus fell apart, the teachings of Moses and the sermons of the prophets were ignored and gradually forgotten. The few remaining members of society who might have provided a nucleus of the religious and cultural stability and continuity could accomplish almost nothing in the chaotic conditions which prevailed. Edomites, Ammonites, Moabites, and others from the neighboring regions—some of whom had previously been settled by Assyria in the territory of the northern kingdom—encroached more and more on the territory of Judah. Inevitably this infiltration led to intermarriage with these alien peoples and then indirectly to their gradually increasing influence upon the religious practices and daily life of the Israelites. Thus with the general tendency toward social and intellectual deterioration, assimilation and syncretism went on apace. Finally Judah, much reduced in territory, came under the control of a governor who resided in Samaria.

The Babylonian Captivity

In Babylonia, the exiled Jews found themselves in the midst of a flourishing and impressive civilization. The Chaldean regime of Nebuchadnezzar (605–562)—currently the greatest power in western Asia—had embarked on a tremendous building campaign for the glorification of the king, his capital, and his empire. Among the new structures were the terraces of Babylon, the so-called Hanging Gardens which the Greeks made famous as one of the seven wonders of the world. In actual fact, these masonary terraces were eclipsed by the Ishtar Gate and by the temple of Marduk built in stepped tiers like the towers of a modern skyscraper. To carry out these projects, artisans of all kinds were imported, both as captives and as highly paid skilled workers, as recorded in the Biblical statement: "And Nebu-

chadnezzar carried away . . . all the craftsmen and smiths"
(II Kings 24:14).

The Judean exiles were treated no differently from the
other captive peoples. The common folk were generally
enslaved outright, and those of higher status were given
limited freedom to earn a living and choose their abode.
A number of the exiled Judeans even managed to live in
their own homes in a special quarter of the city of Babylon.

Especially interesting is the manner in which the Biblical
and the Babylonian texts confirm and clarify one another
in their statements about the Babylonian treatment of King
Jehoiachin and his household. The Biblical historian tells
us:

And in the thirty-seventh year of the exile of Jehoiachin king
of Judah . . . Evil-merodach king of Babylon, in the year that
he began to reign, lifted up the head of Jehoiachin king of
Judah from prison. And he spoke kindly to him, and gave him
a seat above the seats of the kings who were with him in
Babylon. And Jehoiachin put off his prison garments, and he
ate regularly in the king's presence all the days of his life. And
for his allowance, a regular allowance was given him by the
king, every day a portion, all the days of his life [II Kings
25:27–30].

Shortly after the beginning of the twentieth century, the
Kaiser Friedrich Museum in Berlin received some three
hundred cuneiform tablets which had been excavated by
a German expedition near the Ishtar Gate in Babylon.
These tablets lay for over three decades in the basement of
the museum, uncleaned and undeciphered. Under the very
thorough Nazi regime, the curator of the museum came
upon the boxes of tablets and began to study them. He was
astounded to discover that several of the tablets dealt

precisely with the same King Jehoiachin of Judah and his family in exile in Babylon, and that these texts not only substantiated but even filled in gaps in the Biblical account. It is unusual for archaeological discoveries to confirm a Biblical account so specifically.

Practically all the Judean exiles, except those who had been enslaved and brutalized by exhausting manual labor, longed for home. As time passed, however, and no immediate prospect of release developed, many were caught up in the colorful life of the Babylonian metropolis. These practical folk, recognizing that life went on in any case, made up their minds to "sing low in a bad tune" and to learn to adjust to Babylonian ways and customs according to the advice of Jeremiah:

Thus says the Lord of Hosts, the God of Israel, to all the exiles whom I have exiled from Jerusalem to Babylon: Build yourselves houses, and dwell in them, and plant gardens, and eat their fruit. Take yourselves wives and have sons and daughters; and take wives for your sons, and give your daughters to husbands, that they may bear sons and daughters; and multiply there and be not diminished. And seek the welfare of the city to which I have exiled you, and pray to the Lord for it; for in its welfare shall you have welfare [29:4 ff].

It should be noted in passing that Jeremiah did not give the Babylonians any credit for having overpowered Judah. The Lord, having condemned Judah, delivered her people to Babylon to serve out their sentence of exile. Thus, according to Jeremiah, the only thing to do was to endure the captivity and build up a record for good behavior.

By about the middle of the sixth century, after some three or four decades, two generations of Judeans had grown up in exile. Those born to families that had sought assimilation had quite lost touch with Judah. For them the memory of Temple and Covenant had faded, and Jerusalem seemed remote and unimportant compared with mighty and cosmopolitan Babylon. Content to earn a living in peace, these people had no desire to return to the land of their fathers and grandfathers.

A minority of the exiles, however, did remain faithful. Consisting largely of priests, Levites, men of learning, landowners, functionaries of the royal administration, and the like, this group maintained the will to resist assimilation. They struggled to keep track of political developments in the world about them and to keep alive the dream of restoring the Temple and the nation of Judah. For them captivity was bitter frustration, and deliverance and return held the one great promise of life, a hope which they implanted and nursed in their children with religious fervor.

The voices of the prophets ceaselessly and tirelessly admonished the expatriates always to remember their origin, their faith, and their mission. These faithful few did not intermarry, or at least not in sufficient numbers to dilute their consciousness of kind. They studied the teachings of Moses and the prophets, and found in them not only the explanation of Judah's defeat and exile, but also a program for salvation and redemption.

The Prophet Ezekiel

Among the Biblical writings which gave expression to this belief, the foremost were the books of Ezekiel and the so-called Second Isaiah. Ezekiel, the first prophet to receive the divine call outside the Holy Land, was visited by God Himself in a vision in Babylonia, and commanded to preach that Judah and the Temple had been overcome not by the might of Babylon, but by the wickedness of Judah which had provoked God's wrath.

Carrying on the great tradition of Jeremiah, Ezekiel contended that the God of Israel was still omnipotent and that Babylon was His mere instrument. Her pomp and might, her lion-guarded ways, her many gods who were "no-gods," all these trappings and appurtenances of power would vanish like mist, once God's anger had run its course. Ezekiel would tolerate no momentary doubt of the inflexible justice of his God, nor would he accept the possibility that God would allow the innocent among the exiled to languish forever and without hope in the same durance with the wicked. With the same fiery faith Ezekiel preached that this punishment that made the bad good, made the good better, and assured, at least ultimately, deliverance for all who obeyed the Lord, observed His Sabbath, and kept themselves from heathen idols and heathen ways.

Ezekiel propounded his basic convictions in the vision of the Valley of Dry Bones (Ezekiel 37), one of the most electrifying passages of the entire Bible. Israel—in this vision—had ceased to be a living nation. Her people had lost faith in God and in themselves. To dramatize their plight, Ezekiel likened them to scattered heaps of bleached bone, lying in a valley. But the Lord, who had brought this terrible curse on His people, promised to bring the dead bones to life, and to restore a unified Israel to its own land under a descendant of King David, saying:

And I will make a covenant of peace with them, and it shall be an everlasting covenant with them; and I will establish them and multiply them, and will set My sanctuary in their midst for ever. . . . And the nations shall know that I the Lord sanctify Israel, when My sanctuary is in their midst for ever" [verses 26–28].

Ezekiel, the first to prophesy after the destruction of Jerusalem, was obsessed by the need to rebuild the Temple. As the abode of the Divine Presence, it was the center of Israelite religious life, the true setting for sacrifice and prayer, for in antiquity no less than nowadays organized religion required a special place for the worship of the Deity. It was natural, therefore, that Ezekiel should also stress the preservation of a strict observance of the Temple ritual. In absolute accord with such exilic and postexilic prophets as the Second Isaiah, Haggai, Zechariah, and Malachi, not to mention his pre-exilic predecessors, Ezekiel warned that ritual laxity led to moral laxity. He and the other prophets of this later era were by no means men of coarser fiber; on the contrary, all of them believed—as firmly as their predecessors—that the efficacy of prayer and sacrifice depended on the worshipper's religious integrity. Their insistence on sacred forms and symbols stemmed not from a willingness to substitute such external tokens for the deeper religious truths but—on the contrary—from their experience that it is infinitely difficult for ordinary men to maintain active religious belief by faith alone.

The Second Isaiah: Babylonian Decline

Ezekiel had never faltered in his convictions of deliverance even during the worst hours of the Exile, but he did not live to see his faith vindicated. Only a few decades after Ezekiel's career came to a close, however, the Babylonian empire began to show great cracks and fissures and, in shorter time than anyone would have believed possible, was on the brink of dissolution. The Persians and Medes had begun to take their place as major powers in the Mesopotamian region late in the seventh century. First the Medes helped the Babylonians crush Assyria and shared in the spoils. Then, about 545, Persia under Cyrus II (the Great) of the Achemenid dynasty absorbed Media, Lydia, and Ionian Greece in Asia Minor. Eventually the new power was to include territories extending all the way from the Indus to the Mediterranean and from the Caucasus to the Indian Ocean, a dominion beside which the conquests of earlier Near Eastern empires pale into insignificance.

During this turbulent period, a great prophet arose to proclaim to his fellow Jews in Babylon that they were entering a new epoch. He is called nowadays the "Second" Isaiah, to distinguish him from the namesake who prophesied in Jerusalem some two hundred years earlier; the writings of this exilic prophet are found in Chapters 40–66 of the Book of Isaiah. They are easily differentiated from those of the First Isaiah by virtue of literary style, historical perspective, and theological emphasis.

Having followed political developments closely, the Second Isaiah realized that even greater events were in the making, and in the swift rise of Persia he sensed the promise of imminent deliverance for Israel. In poetic sermons rarely equaled for pathos and lyricism, he compared the Babylonian Exile with Israel's bondage in Egypt and urged his conviction that even the Exodus would be surpassed by the new liberation and return, a triumph that would be consecrated in a new covenant between God and His people Israel. The one necessary condition, the unknown prophet of the Exile warned, was that the Judean exiles have complete faith in the ability and desire of the Lord to accomplish the restoration.

More than any other prophet since the days of Elijah, the Second Isaiah emphasized and reiterated the uniqueness and omnipotence of the God of Israel. He set himself the task of convincing his fellow Jews that the Babylonians and their gods were not victors over the Judeans and the Lord their God, but that, on the contrary, the heathen were no more than the rod of His anger and chastisement. God was the one ruler in the entire universe, and there was no one else beside Him:

> I am the Lord, that is My name,
>   And My glory I will not give to another
>   Nor My praise to graven images [42:8].

This concept of a universal and omnipotent God was new, of course, only in emphasis. It stemmed in direct line from the teachings of Elijah and Amos, and had been eloquently expressed by the otherwise unknown "man of God" who said to King Ahab of Israel (ninth century):

Thus says the Lord: Because the Arameans have said, "The Lord is a God of the mountains, but He is not a God of the valleys," therefore I will deliver all this great multitude into your hand, and you shall know that I am the Lord [I Kings 20:28].

But as Ezekiel stressed the role of the lost Temple in the worship of the Lord and made its rebuilding a central object of faith, so the Second Isaiah emphasized the universal aspect of God, in his efforts to explain to his fellow Judeans their exile in the foreign land of a great empire which had destroyed the Temple of their God and carried them captive from His land.

The Second Isaiah, realizing that Babylonia was a mere shell of its former greatness, and that Persia was now the dominant power in the Near East, warned his listeners that they had little time to prepare themselves for the destruction of Babylon by God's "shepherd" and "anointed," Cyrus of Persia (Isaiah 44:28; 45:1), and for their liberation and return to Judah.

Cyrus of Persia and the Edict of Liberation

About 540 B.C. Babylonia fell like a ripe fruit into the hands of Persia's king. In his first regnal year (about 538) Cyrus issued the famous Edict of Liberation:

Thus says Cyrus king of Persia: All the kingdoms of the earth has the Lord, the God of heaven, given me; and He has charged me to build Him a house in Jerusalem, which is in Judah. Whosoever there is among you of all His people—his God be with him—let him go up to Jerusalem" [Ezra 1:2-3; II Chronicles 36:22-23].

And he added:

Concerning the house of God at Jerusalem, let the house be built, the place where they offer sacrifices, and let its foundation be strongly laid. Its height shall be sixty cubits, and its width sixty cubits, with three rows of great stones and a row of new timber; and let the expenses be paid out of the king's house. And also let the gold and silver vessels of the house of God, which Nebuchadnezzar took out of the Temple which is in Jerusalem and brought to Babylon, be restored and brought back to the Temple which is in Jerusalem, every one to its place. And you shall put them in the house of God [Ezra 6:3-5].

Sheshbazzar, apparently of the family of King Jehoiachin of Judah, was appointed governor of Judah. Taking with him the sacred vessels of the Temple, Sheshbazzar went to Jerusalem to take up his post and prepared to lay the foundations for the new Temple.

Developments in Judah

But the Judean homeland, devastated and impoverished by Babylonia, was in no condition to support a significant restoration. Many Judeans in Babylonia failed to take advantage of the new liberty to return to Judah. The majority, having adapted themselves well enough to their new home, lacked the necessary incentive to start all over again in a much poorer land. As for the many who had never been forced into exile, few evinced any enthusiasm for rebuilding the Temple and for recapturing a way of life long since abandoned. Nearly twenty years after Cyrus' edict, the prophet Haggai condemned the Judeans for their inertia, saying bitterly, "Is it a time for you yourselves to dwell in your paneled houses, while this House lies in ruins?" (1:4). When drought and famine came upon the land, Haggai insisted that the hardships were a manifestation of God's displeasure at the people's failure to rebuild His Temple. The prophet Zechariah, too, castigated the people for their apathy.

The foreigners who had poured into Judah during the Exile saw the restoration of the Temple as a threat to their position and prosperity, and, accordingly, opposed it. Among those of mixed marriages, the attitudes ranged from complete indifference to a willingness to back the projects; but when some of this mixed population, chiefly the Samaritans, volunteered their assistance, their offer was rejected and they were denounced as idolators (Ezra 4:1–4, 24; 5–6).

During this period, Zerubbabel, of the family of King Jehoiachin and the House of David, was the civil head of the community, and Joshua the high priest was recognized leader of the priestly group. Haggai and Zechariah had envisaged a restoration of Judah under a scion of the House of David, with a free priesthood in full charge of the Temple and religious matters.

It was, however, the representatives of the religious rather than the civil authority who finally came to power. Cambyses II, son and successor of Cyrus, committed suicide in 522 B.C., and for a brief interval the Persian empire faltered. During the confusion, several of the subject provinces revolted, creating the impression among some of the Judeans still at home—Haggai and Zechariah among them —that the end of the empire was at hand. Jumping at what they took to be a chance to restore Judah's independence at one blow, they named Zerubbabel God's chosen one, thus declaring independence of Persia (Haggai 2:20–23). The priestly group seems to have been more cautious. And their caution was rewarded when Darius I (522–486 B.C.), crushed the widespread rebellion and re-established the imperial rule.

Just how Zerubbabel and his backers fared during this troubled interlude is not known, but the movement is never heard of again. Led by Haggai and Joshua, however, the Judeans perserved in their efforts to rebuild the Temple. The Persian government, in accordance with its general policy of supporting local priesthoods, ignored the objections of its own governor, Tattenai, and of the anti-Jewish section of the population, and granted the Jews permission to continue with the work. About 516 B.C. the second Temple was dedicated, just seventy years after the first had been destroyed. Judah now became a theocracy, under Persian rule, with Joshua the high priest at its head.

Little is known about the happenings in Judea during the earlier part of the fifth century. The Persian government continued its policy of granting its colonies, Judea included, a considerable degree of religious and cultural autonomy, keeping at the same time a firm hold on military, economic, and political affairs. The Jewish community in Judea grew in numbers and in prosperity only gradually, and while it seems to have taken good care of the Temple, it permitted the walls of Jerusalem, destroyed by Nebuchadnezzar's army, to remain in ruins. At the same time, intermarriage between the Judeans and the gentiles continued, and their assimilation progressed.

The Jewries of Egypt and Persia

Elsewhere in the Persian empire Jews were involved in two revealing incidents. It will be remembered that when Nebuchadnezzar's forces were overrunning Judah, and again when the Judeans revolted—to their sorrow—against Gedaliah, some of the populace sought asylum in Egypt. About sixty years later (c. 525 B.C.) the Persians incorporated Egypt in their empire, whereupon some of the expatriate Jews there volunteered for military service with the conqueror, and were assigned to garrison duty.

The sudden reappearance of Jews in Egyptian history is recorded by the Elephantine Papyri, ancient documents of a Jewish military colony at the city of Elephantine, just below the first cataract of the Nile. Written in Aramaic —the "language of diplomacy and trade throughout western Asia in the Persian period, and which was gradually replacing Hebrew as the everyday tongue of the Jewish

people not only abroad, but also at home in Palestine"—
the Elephantine Papyri constitute a prime source for the
reconstruction of Egyptian and Jewish history and throw
important side lights on the colonial history of Persia as
well. They indicate, for example, that the imperial rule of
the Persian government was generally liberal, at least in
comparison with the naked despotism of her predecessors,
Egypt, Babylon, and Assyria.

The Jewish colony was allowed its own temple where
sacrifices were regularly offered up to God and around
which the colony's activities revolved. The business con-
tracts and other documents among the Papyri indicate that
the Jews bought and sold land and houses, married and
divorced, and, in general, lived a normal life. There is
evidence that some Jews intermarried with the Egyptians
and became more or less assimilated in the religious and
social life of the country. The community as a whole, however, appears to have retained a distinct character. For
one thing, it was organized along military lines, with
Persians and Babylonians normally in command of the
larger units. Then too, the Jews, unlike the native Egyptians, employed Aramaic as their official language. Finally
the Jewish colonists, genuinely appreciative of the Persian
colonial policy and their privileged position in the imperial
organization, were the most loyal subjects that Persia had.

On several occasions the Egyptians revolted against their
Persian conquerors. In one of these uprisings, during the
reign of Darius II (about 410), a mob incited by the local
priests and merchants attacked and looted the Jewish temple
in the first anti-Jewish pogrom on record. The motivation
behind this directed outburst of violence—which the Persian authorities quickly suppressed and punished—appears

to have been a combination of two related factors. First, the Egyptian upper classes sought to divert the social discontent among the general population against an alien religious group which could also be identified with Persian imperialism. Second, the Egyptian priests and merchants hoped to exploit the general social discontent to weaken and, if possible, to destroy their economic rivals in the Jewish community.

The Book of Esther describes a similar incident, this time at Susa, at the eastern end of the Persian empire. A certain Haman, the highest official in the regime of King Ahasuerus—perhaps one of the Xerxes kings—persuaded his master to hand over to him for destruction and spoil the Jews of Susa and of the empire. Haman pointed out that the Jews were unassimilable, and that "their laws are diverse from those of every people" (Esther 3:8). Indeed, Haman argued, it was "not to the king's profit to tolerate them," and for the privilege of stripping them—which would be a public service—he offered to pay ten thousand talents of silver. In spite of the extraordinary offer Haman was thwarted by Ahasuerus' favorite, the Jewess Esther (Hadassah). Under the guidance of her wise cousin, Mordecai, she caused Haman to be hanged from his own gallows and his henchmen killed. But the Jews, in their turn, "did not stretch forth their hand to the spoil" of the Persians (3:11, 13; 9:15–16).

The Book of Esther, as so many critics have pointed out, is much too pat and wishfully contrived to be accepted as simple historical fact. Yet the account, however much idealized, follows closely, in essence, the objective chronicle of the Elephantine Papyri, and may therefore safely be considered as a reflection of fact. It seems more than likely

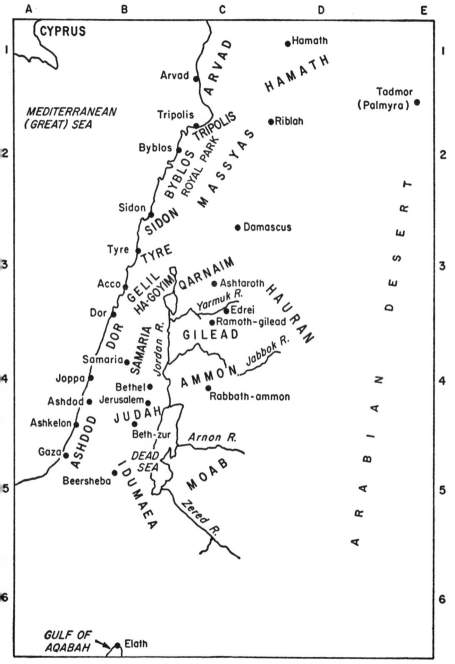

V. The restoration under Ezra and Nehemiah (fifth and fourth centuries B.C.).

that under the Achemenid regime expatriate Jews achieved positions of wealth and influence, not only in Egypt but throughout the Persian empire, and that this personal prosperity produced the usual inimical repercussions engendered by minority success—which would account for the story of Esther, or pogrom narrowly averted.

Among the Jews, the triumph of Esther came to be observed in the joyous feast of Purim, which recalls

the days wherein the Jews had rest from their enemies, and the month was turned for them from sorrow to gladness, and from mourning to a good day; that they should make them days of feasting and gladness, and of sending choice portions one to another, and gifts to the poor [9:22].

After the destruction of Judah and the Temple, and the subsequent exile, it was natural for a people to celebrate joyfully such a narrow and triumphant escape from great disaster.

Ezra and Nehemiah

To return to Judah—or Judea, to keep its new status clear—the decisive turn toward national as well as religious revival came about in the time of Ezra the Scribe and Nehemiah. Just when Ezra lived is unknown—even whether he preceded, was contemporary with, or followed Nehemiah. But their combined influence on the history of Judea during the latter half of the fifth and the first decades of the fourth centuries is made abundantly clear in the Biblical text.

An important person in the Jewish community of Babylon and highly regarded by the Persian government, Ezra, "the priest and scribe of the Law of the God of heaven," was authorized by King Artaxerxes to proceed to Jerusalem and there, with the assistance of the king's officials, to reorganize the entire Jewish community in accordance with the Law of Moses (Ezra 7:12–26).

Ezra brought back with him to Judea the various compilations which recorded the early traditions of the patriarchal and Mosaic period, substantially the Five Books of Moses as preserved today. Chapter 8 of Nehemiah describes the dramatic scene in Jerusalem when the entire adult Jewish population gathered to hear Ezra read and explain to them the text of the Torah, the Law of Moses. Rabbi Jose of Palestine (second century A.D.) justly expressed the importance of Ezra, even in comparison with Moses, in the establishment of the Torah as the basis of Judaism, when he said, "Ezra was worthy of having the Law given through him to Israel, had not Moses preceded him."

One of the important consequences of the official adoption of the Torah, in addition to the renewed observance of such holy days as the feasts of Tabernacles (Succoth) and Passover, was the decision of Ezra to order every Jew to divorce his gentile wife. This was a far-reaching decision, and not an easy one to carry out. Opposition to this move came from every walk of Jewish life, and it found expression in the Book of Ruth. The author of this beautiful little novel expressed the opinion that no gentile who became a sincere convert to Judaism, such as Ruth the Moabitess, should be cast out or denied.

This attitude would not ordinarily have been rejected; but in this period intermarriage had become so extensive, and the consequences so detrimental to the Jews as God's people, that Ezra and his followers could no longer accept the results in silence. It should be noted, in this connection, too, that the author of Ruth did not favor Judean missionary

activity among the gentiles. Biblical Israel was not evangel-
ical, and genuine voluntary conversion to Judaism was at
most condoned.

While maintaining the policy of continued loyalty to
Persia, Ezra led a social and religious revival in Judea. At
about this time some Jews began to rebuild the walls of
Jerusalem. This prompted the governor of Samaria, under
whose administration Judea lay, to notify King Artaxerxes
that the Jews were planning to revolt. The king at once
ordered the work stopped. Nehemiah, a loyal cup-bearer
in the royal court and an ardent supporter of the restoration of Jerusalem as a religious symbol and center, hearing
of the order, pleaded to be allowed to supervise the work
himself, vowing that he would proceed in such a way that
the imperial interest would not be jeopardized. "If it
please the king," he begged, "and if your servant has found
favor in your sight, send me to Judah, to the city of my
fathers' sepulchres, that I may build it" (Nehemiah 2:5).

Artaxerxes was persuaded, and Nehemiah went to Judea
taking with him full credentials and authority. As would
be expected, Nehemiah's extraordinary powers aroused bitter opposition in Judea. Sanballat, governor of Samaria and
Nehemiah's superior, and Tobiah, governor of Ammon,
accused Nehemiah of plotting a revolt against the king.
Geshem the Arab, perhaps the governor of Dedan in Arabia,
"whom it grieved greatly that someone had come to seek
the welfare of the children of Israel" (2:19), also took
umbrage. Geshem became embroiled in the Judean situation
because of his fear of a commercial revival to the north,
which would have put him back in the same disadvantageous
position that Arabia's Queen of Sheba had occupied in
relation to Israel's King Solomon.

Nehemiah, however, was not deterred, nor did the Persian central government withdraw its support. The walls of Jerusalem, the Bible tells us, were restored in fifty-two days of heroic effort, as Nehemiah had boasted would happen in his prophetic defiance: "The God of heaven will succeed for us; and we His servants, we will arise and we will build. And you will have no portion or right or memorial in Jerusalem" (2:20). The builders "did the work with one hand and held a weapon in the other," we are told in a passage (Nehemiah 4:11 ff.; 4:17 ff. in the English versions) that recalls the rebuilding of modern Israel.

As had so often happened before in Judea, improving fortune brought a corresponding increase of social inequity. Once again the upper-class Judeans enriched themselves at the expense of the poor. The moneylenders tightened their fists, the common folk began to lose their land and property, serfdom reappeared. "We are forcing our sons and daughters to become slaves," the people complained to Nehemiah: "Some of our daughters have been enslaved, and we cannot help it, for other men possess our fields and our vineyards" (5:1 ff.).

The heavy tribute paid to Persia by Judea further aggravated the situation because the well to do industriously foisted onto the common people as large a share as possible of this collective obligation. To correct the serious dislocation, Nehemiah attempted to force the rich to take an oath guaranteeing the return of mortgaged properties and goods held under pledge to their owners. This act of social justice, which may possibly have been a political move to win mass support for the theocratic party, provoked the Persian overseers to recall Nehemiah to Shushan.

During his absence, religious conditions in Jerusalem deteriorated. Tobiah the Ammonite had set up living quarters in the court of the Temple. Many of the levitical and priestly workers had left the Temple because they were not being supported by its revenues. The Sabbath was being violated, by Jews as well as by local Tyrian merchants. Intermarriage between Jews and the gentile populations of Ashdod, Ammon, and Moab again increased, and the children were being raised in ignorance of their Jewish faith and of the Hebrew language.

When the zealot, Nehemiah, finally returned to Jerusalem, he wasted no time in throwing out Tobiah. He appointed honest treasurers and restored the Temple staff to full complement. Breakers of the Sabbath laws were arrested and punished. And those who dared flout the ban on intermarriage were fined, cursed, and made to take an oath that never would they permit their issue to marry a gentile. Nehemiah ended his remarkable memoirs with the plea, "Remember me, O my God, for good."

The Jewish Theocratic State

The historical legacy of Ezra and Nehemiah was the theocratic state of Judea. The Persian Royal administration and the High Priest of Judah represented the upper class, the practical work of administration being done by the civil service, temple bureaucracies, and the judiciary. The urban and rural population, especially the peasantry, who supported the entire structure, accepted the Mosaic Law and priestly control, in the belief that their well-being was thus assured.

The Jewish theocratic state was strong enough to withstand the various forces of opposition, both domestic and international, which beset her. Thus Sanballat of Samaria built a temple on Mount Gerizim for his son-in-law, Manasseh, grandson of Eliashib the high priest of Jerusalem. This Samaritan shrine and its adherents became in time a festering sore to the Jews of Judea.

The administrative and religious bureaucracies fought constantly for power. On one occasion (about 400), Bagoas, the governor of Judea, threatened to dismiss Jonathan, the high priest, in favor of the latter's brother, Joshua. Jonathan murdered Joshua in the Temple, and Bagoas used this as a pretext to interfere with the Temple services and the priestly prerogatives.

A pattern of Judaism was being woven in Judea while the Persian empire at large was beginning to show signs of disintegration. The history of the Jewish people, shaped largely by the priests during the rest of the Persian period, was soon to enter a new stage, in the hellenistic period, when the theocratic state was replaced by a commonwealth, and when the Torah constitution was reinterpreted by the liberal Pharisees in accordance with the new conditions. The Judaism which the Pharisees developed maintained a profound influence on all phases of Jewish life during the more than two thousand years which followed and is a potent factor in Judaism and in Israel today.

CHAPTER VII

The Hebraic Spirit: The Prophetic Movement and Social Justice

THE prophetic movement forms the climax of Biblical history. Nothing comparable was produced by any of the other Near Eastern civilizations of antiquity. Its influence has followed the spread of, and dominated the development of, the three great world religions, Judaism, Christianity, and Islam, to such extent that for twenty centuries, over nearly half the land surface of the globe, the consciences of civilized men have spoken with the accents of the prophets. The socialists of the nineteenth century, who scorned all revealed religion, acknowledged the prophets as the first social reformers and the source of their own new doctrine. Even rationalist and skeptical scholars of the period, who rejected nearly every part of the Bible as unhistorical, recognized the greatness of the prophets, the validity of their teaching, and the power of their eloquence.

The Rise of the Prophetic Movement

The Hebrew word for "prophet" is *nabi*, but its original meaning is not known. It would seem that *nabi* in the Bible means approximately "spokesman," as when the Lord told

Moses, "Aaron your brother shall be your spokesman (*nabi*)" (Exodus 7:1; compare "shall be your mouth" in 4:16). That is how the Jews themselves translated *nabi*—in the oldest Greek translation of the Pentateuch, the Septuagint, about 200 B.C.; and the Greek word which was there employed, *prophetes*, "declarer" or "interpreter," is the source of the English word "prophet." It even appears that the word "prophet" in English meant simply "forth-teller" or "preacher" as late as the time of Queen Elizabeth; the meaning "foretelling," "predicting," is a later development. The prophet spoke for God, and interpreted His word and will to his fellow Israelites.

The prophetic movement in Israel developed in two distinct stages. In the earlier phase, the Biblical prophets were essentially no different from the diviners common to the ancient Near East in general. In fact, the Bible itself states explicitly, in an editorial gloss at I Samuel 9:9, "Previously in Israel, when a person went to inquire of God, thus he said, 'Come, let us go to the seer'; for he who is now called a prophet was previously called a seer." Samuel the prophet was called a "seer" and "a man of God." And in II Samuel 24:11 we read that "the word of the Lord came to the prophet Gad, David's visionary [or, seer]."

Soothsayers, seers, miracle workers—that is, people who divined by magic formula, who gave out oracular utterances, who professed expertness in transmitting the supernatural—were a definite social group in the ancient civilizations of the Near East. Ecstasy, frenzy, the examination of the liver and entrails of animals, the flight of birds, the interpretation of dreams, astrology, the casting of lots, divination by water—all these were the property and trademark of the priestly and related guilds from the Euphrates to the Nile. For the seers of antiquity were organized in guilds, which had set rules governing masters and apprentices, as surely as if they were stonemasons. These craftsmen in the supernatural worked both in groups and as individuals.

Cuneiform texts recently discovered at Mari, dating from the eighteenth century B.C., illustrate this earlier stage in Biblical prophecy. One describes how a deputation of priests advises the king to pay more attention to the gods that they represent and to the sanctuary that they make it their business to tend. Another text, this one from Egypt and dating back to about 1100 B.C., illustrates how holy men resorted to states of frenzy in order to "divine."

Such seizures and frenzies are reported of Biblical prophecy in its formative stage, often in a context which suggests the existence of recognized soothsayer or seer groups specializing in the invocation of hysterical trances. For example, shortly after Saul was anointed king by Samuel, he ran into a "band of prophets coming down from the shrine, led by harp, tambourine, flute, and lyre . . . and the spirit of God rushed upon him, and he prophesied among them" (I Samuel 10:5–12). In fact, it seems probable that the early prophets were all to some degree professional soothsayers. Several, Nathan, Gad, and Iddo, for example, were attached to the royal court, just as the priests, the tax-collectors, the commander-in-chief of the army, and other royal functionaries. Others, like Samuel of Ramah and Ahijah of Shiloh, were attached to sanctuaries outside of Jerusalem; and in this early stage, they frequently worked in groups. Samuel himself was head of such a "band of prophets" as Saul had met (19:20). In the days of Elijah and Elisha there is frequent mention of groups of prophets of the Lord, among them the groups located at Jericho and Bethel. On another occasion four hundred "prophets of the Lord" were summoned by Jehoshaphat of Judah and the king of Israel to interpret God's will in regard to an attack on Ramoth-gilead (I Kings 22:6). This incident recalls the 450 prophets of Baal and the 400 prophets of Asherah who contested with Elijah's God on Mount Carmel (I Kings 18).

Among the earlier prophets, it was also characteristic to transmit the craft from generation to generation. Elijah trained Elisha and invested him as his successor (II Kings 2, a dramatic chapter), and before them, Jehu the prophet was the father of Hanani the seer (I Kings 16:1, 7; II Chronicles 16:7–10). Likewise, nearly all performed miracles, as Moses did before Pharaoh to convince him that the God of the Hebrews was supreme. Samuel was a seer; and the prophets Elijah and Elisha freely worked miracles of various kinds.

From Miracle to Rhapsody

In the eighth century, however, divination and miracle working were virtually eliminated from the prophetic tradition in Israel. Seers such as Samuel and miracle workers like Elijah and Elisha ceased to be the norm. The ecstatic element continued, but the prophets began to utilize and perfect another medium by which to convince their fellow Israelites of the truth of their teachings. To achieve this effect they began to rely more and more on the eloquence and logic of their literary compositions.

The development from the miracle-working to the rhapsodic stage of prophecy was not peaceful and evolutionary. The literary prophets were opposed to the prophetic guilds, to the practice of prophecy as a craft, and to the idea that any person could be taught by the masters how to "prophesy."

There is no evidence that any of the later literary prophets functioned in groups or that they were heads or members of guilds or that they trained disciples. They were not representatives of any court or sanctuary, nor did they practice prophecy as a regular occupation or a way to earn a living. Instead, they felt themselves inspired directly by God, and only when God and the occasion demanded, as Amos insisted (in the eighth century): "For the Lord God does nothing without revealing His counsel to His servants the prophets. . . . The Lord God has spoken, who can help but prophesy!" (3:7–8). Thus when the chief priest at Bethel contemptuously dismissed Amos and told him to go back to his native Judah to make a living there from his craft, Amos was stung to protest, "I am not a [professional] prophet nor a member of a prophetic guild [literally, the son of a prophet]; but I am a herdsman, and a dresser of sycamore trees" (7:12 ff.). In time, the literary prophets came to scorn the priests—who had become little more than functionaries of the royal court—and the various groups of prophets—whom they called "false prophets"—and they saw only themselves as the true spokesmen of God.

Although it should not be overlooked that several of the earlier prophets had produced important literary compositions, the later prophets fully merit the characterization of "literary" or "rhapsodic," to distinguish them from their predecessors. This title, however, must not be allowed to obscure the far more important fact that this elevation of style reflects a sublimated moral and religious experience,

free from the least trace of magic. It is this elevated character which fundamentally distinguishes the "literary"
prophets from their precursors.

The Prophetic Concept of Social Justice:
The Covenant and the Law

The prophets, the earlier as well as the later, took their
stand on two fundamental ideas: first, that there was a
Covenant between God and His people Israel and, second,
that this Covenant bound the Israelites to a just relationship one to the other. It will be recalled that the patriarchs,
individually, had entered into the Covenant with God that
they would worship Him alone and that He would protect
them. This personal Covenant was broadened in the period
of Moses, as a consequence of the Exodus from Egypt, so
that the entire population of Israel became God's chosen
people to recognize and serve Him as the only God in the
world. This Covenant, it should be noted carefully, was
voluntary on both sides. God elected Israel in His love and
grace, and Israel freely undertook to carry out the will of
God.

According to the prophets, God agreed, for His part, to
reward His faithful people in the land of Israel with
economic prosperity, good health, and peace from all enemies (Deuteronomy 7:12 ff.; and elsewhere). When Israel
prospered, therefore, it could be assumed that her people
had found favor in the sight of the Lord, and prophetic
activity was consequently at a minimum. When, however,
a difficulty arose or threatened to appear, it was a sure sign
that Israel had transgressed against the Covenant and that
God was punishing His people. It was in such times of

crisis and distress that the prophets undertook to determine and expound the reasons for God's anger and the ways by which the Covenant could be restored.

Since it was not possible for God Himself to transgress the Covenant, the prophets necessarily sought the causes of conflict in the actions of the people. When the leaders or the common folk had worshiped other gods, as in the case of King Manasseh (II Kings 21), the prophets denounced those who practiced or tolerated this abomination. Far more often, however, Israelites broke the Covenant in their relations one with another, and it was such lapses that most frequently provoked the prophets' wrath.

The first obligation laid on the Israelites by the Covenant and the Law was the worship of the Lord with prayer and sacrifice. The prophets deemed these formal aspects of worship both necessary and good, but they regarded them as valueless unless fraught with sincerity which found expression in daily conduct. Isaiah would not accept lip service as a substitute for active faith and an upright life. He warns on behalf of God in the majestic first chapter of his book:

Bring no more false offerings. Sacrifice is an abomination to Me. . . . I cannot endure iniquity along with the solemn assembly. . . . Even when you make many prayers, I will not hear. . . . Wash yourselves, make yourselves clean; put away your evil doings from before My eyes. Cease to do evil. Learn to do good. Seek justice. Relieve the oppressed. Take up the case for the fatherless. Plead for the widow.

The prophets, from first to last, demanded with stubborn insistence that the people bring their practices to conform with their beliefs. The teachings of the Lord, epitomized in the Torah, the Law of Moses, did not lead to salvation unless put into daily use. When Saul disobeyed God's command to destroy all the flocks and herds of the Amalekites and instead offered up the choicest animals as a sacrifice, Samuel is reported to have rebuked him. Jeremiah denounced mere lip service and empty ritual time and time again, and on one occasion proclaimed:

Thus says the Lord of Hosts, the God of Israel: Add your burnt offerings to your sacrifices, and eat the flesh. For I did not speak to your fathers nor command them in the day that I brought them out of the land of Egypt concerning burnt offerings and sacrifices. But this thing I commanded them, saying, "Obey My voice, and I will be your God, and you shall be My people, and walk in all the way that I command you, that it may be well with you" [7:21–23].

Nowhere else but in ancient Israel has there been found such persistent and insistent emphasis on doing, on carrying out, not merely on believing in, the teachings of God's spokesmen. That is why Micah was able to put in so few words the essence of Biblical Judaism when he said:

It has been shown to you. O man, what is good
    and what the Lord requires of you:
Only to do justice
    and to love loyally
    and to walk humbly with your God [6:8].

This basic principle, that the law had to be obeyed in spirit together with the letter, was summed up even more succinctly in Deuteronomy 16:20, in the three Hebrew words *Tsédek tsédek tirdof*, "Justice, justice shall you pursue." Salvation by faith alone, or by deeds alone, was an unknown doctrine in the Bible; the letter was inseparable from the spirit, even as the act was inseparable from the

faith. The insistence on this point may well have arisen
from the fact that, difficult as it is to judge the depth and
sincerity of purely religious devotion, the justice of a man's
acts to his fellows was immediately and inescapably apparent in the small tribal society within which the people
of Israel lived. When a merchant was discovered cheating
a customer in weighing or measuring, his act was regarded
not merely as a civil offense against a fellow Israelite,
but much worse as a breach of the Covenant and an abomination of the Lord (Deuteronomy 25:13–16; Leviticus
19:35–37). This sense of equality before the law, moreover, was so strong that a special warning had to be issued
that care should be taken that a person not be favored in
court merely because he was poor, any more than one be
favored because of his wealth: "Justly shall you judge
your neighbor" (Leviticus 19:15).

All the prophets considered all the Israelites to be equal
before the Covenant and in the sight of God, be he king
or priest, master or servant, rich or poor. This inherent
equality imposed on everyone the personal and inescapable
obligation to hear, understand, and obey the divine law. To
the prophets, therefore, every act of injustice on the part
of one Israelite to another, or of one group against another,
was a transgression against the Covenant and necessarily
brought on punishment. The function of the prophets was
to discern such iniquities in whatever form, and to persuade
the transgressors to repent their sins and to return to God.
This equality before the Covenant raised all Israelites to
the common dignity of participating in the Covenant with
God.

The injunction upon each Israelite to deal justly with
his fellows thereby became more than the defense of

rights of property or persons; it became a defense of human dignity. Thus, if a man was to be lashed in punishment for a crime, then the maximum number of stripes was to be forty, "lest, if he should continue to be struck many stripes above these, your brother should be degraded in your presence" (Deuteronomy 25:1–3). And if the law forbade the gleaning of the vineyard and commanded that "it should be for the sojourner, the fatherless and the widow," it was expressly pointed out that God did so because He wanted the Israelites to remember that they too were once helpless slaves, in Egypt (24:21–22).

It has long been recognized that law played an extremely important part in the life of Israel, but even so, sufficient attention has not always been paid to the essential nature of Israel's laws. They established not only the code of conduct for all Israelites in dealing one with another—and especially the relations between members of the ruling classes and the less powerful—but through this code gave expression to the obligation for just and righteous behavior inherent in the Covenant. The prophets, more than any other group, emphasized the fact that the laws expressed God's will or, as one Psalmist said in praise of God and His Covenant: "Righteousness and justice are the foundation of Your throne, steadfast love and truth go before You" (Psalm 89:15).

Although the prophets are now usually recognized as the greatest source of inspiration for doctrines of social reform, they were nevertheless reformers within, rather than of, their social system. They supported the existing order and concentrated all their magnificent indignation on the need to infuse the observance of ritual and legal regulations with spiritual integrity and a deep sense of moral justice. It was this emphasis on the spirit of the law which at once provoked the prophets to their greatest denunciations and exhortations and at the same time brought them into conflict with the privileged members of their society. As has generally been the way of the rich and powerful, the privileged Israelites frequently succumbed to the temptation to use the law to their advantage; and while insisting most vehemently on the literal observance of ritual and legality, they often failed most significantly to live up to the highest standards implied in the Covenant. It was failings of this sort that provided the prophets with the texts for their most eloquent sermons.

Thus it was not social inequality but social injustice which they denounced, not the existence of rich and poor within the same society but the abuse of the poor by their richer brethren which they decried, not the creation of a new society but the infusion of the Israel they knew with a new spirit which they demanded. Their basic social philosophy rested on the conviction that if the people expressed their faith in God by obeying His commandments in their hearts as well as in their acts, the moral climate of Israel would be purified and the life of her society would be sound.

The alternative was clear. Transgression of justice and rejection of God's will were sure to be followed by swift and terrible punishment meted out by God Himself. Innumerable examples of this divine retribution are recorded in the Bible. Indeed, the frequency with which the prophetic warnings of doom were fulfilled revived, later on, the concept that God's spokesmen were foretellers or that they had the power to call down upon the hapless sinner the curse of heaven. To the prophets themselves, however, neither attribution was justified. Punishment was ordained by God, and the recognition that it would follow injustice was not a secret to be divined by a seer but rather the inescapable conclusion of the Covenant.

The Fate of the Prophets and Their Teachings

It was the fate of the prophets, however, that even within this limited context their teachings were not put into practice. The majestic simplicity and vigor of their language, together with their unswerving concentration on the basic elements of the Hebrew faith and moral code, made it all but impossible for their exhortations to be ignored. When, however, a prophet's denunciation of wrongdoing too strongly swayed the oppressed—if not the oppressors—the ruling classes frequently were forced to pay lip service to the prophetic message in order to maintain or strengthen their hold on the people. Thus the writings of Amos were accepted, to become part of Holy Writ, and used by the secular and priestly rulers to strengthen the institutions of law and public worship. Similarly, the so-called Reformation of Josiah, which Jeremiah first supported enthusiastically, provided one more occasion for the use of prophetic teachings in the special interests of the monarchy and the priesthood of Jerusalem. Vehemently, as the prophets demanded the substance of justice for the orphan and the widow, for the weak and the oppressed, the laws of the kingdom continued to punish ritual transgression more regularly and more severely than moral injustice.

One of the outstanding characteristics of the prophets was the forthrightness and conviction with which they addressed themselves to those Israelites, without the least regard for their rank or power, who flouted or perverted the law. Through this uncompromising vehemence, the prophets continually risked and sometimes suffered abuse and even death at the hands of those they attacked. Indeed, believing that all Israelites were equal before the Covenant and in the sight of the Lord, the prophets could hardly have done otherwise than denounce the iniquities of the strong with the same freedom and vigor as those of the weak, and when they suffered it was for their fierce love of the inexorable justice of their God.

Nathan did not hesitate to denounce David the mighty king for his murderous action against Uriah the Hittite (II Samuel 12). Elijah had to flee for his life because of his vehement denunciations of Ahab and Jezebel. Micaiah was hit on the cheek and thrown into prison (I Kings 22:24–27). Amos the Judean risked limb and life when he audaciously invaded the royal sanctuary at Bethel and told the royal house and its supporters what lay in store for them as retribution for their rebellion against the Lord. Because Jeremiah bitterly denounced the domestic and foreign policy of his government, his life was threatened, he was beaten, he was put in stocks, and he was thrown into a dungeon, so that he was constrained to cry out, "And I was like a docile lamb that is led to the slaughter" (11:19). The Second Isaiah echoed these words when he described himself "as a lamb that is led to the slaughter, and as a sheep that is dumb before her shearers" (53:7). Ezekiel was told by God, "And you, son of man, be not afraid of them, neither be afraid of their words, though briers and thorns be with you and you dwell among scorpions" (Ezekiel 2:6). Uriah the prophet was killed by King Jehoiakim (Jeremiah 26:20–23), and the prophet Zechariah was stoned to death (II Chronicles 24:20–21).

Read in a later time and under wholly altered circumstances, these sufferings were interpreted as expiatory sacrifices meekly accepted by the prophets to atone for the iniquities of their people, and the prophetic insistence on the equality of all before the Covenant was interpreted as belief in a universality encompassing not merely the children of Israel but all men of all nations.

In the great prophecies of doom one of the most common and impressive themes is the warning to the Israelites that unless they hearken to the word of the Lord they would suffer defeat and even conquest at the hands of their enemies. Thus in the reigns of Jehoiakim, Jehoiachin, and Zedekiah (about 608–586 B.C.), a powerful section of the Judean ruling class wanted to make a pact with Egypt and other countries against Babylonia. Jeremiah, however, condemned this move as contrary to the will of God and therefore a step toward certain disaster. Instead, he urged a policy of continued co-operation with Babylonia (e.g., Jeremiah 25–29).

The same pattern is evident over a century earlier, about 735 B.C., when Isaiah analyzed the efforts of King Pekah of Israel and King Rezin of Aram to force Judah into a coalition against the expanding Assyrian empire (Isaiah 7–8). The prophet advised Judah's government to avoid any such alliance, warning that Israel and her Aramean ally would surely fall. "Behold," he said,

a young woman is with child and shall bear a son, and shall call his name Immanuel. . . . And before the child knows how to refuse the evil and choose the good, the land before whose two kings you are in dread will be deserted" [7:14 ff.].

The historical context makes it clear that the prophets were, in fact, analyzing with extraordinary acumen the

balance of forces in the world of the Levant and urging
their conclusions upon their fellow Israelites with the majestic eloquence of their tradition. Read in this light, the
reference to the young woman and her child becomes nothing more than a dramatic measure of time, a warning that
before the unborn child will be old enough to know the
difference between good and evil, the Lord will bring
devastation on Judah's enemies (compare 8:1–4). Yet when
passages of this sort were read in a later and wholly different
set of conditions they laid the basis for the common belief
that the prophets were foretellers and that their gift was
based not merely on their power of analysis of an immediate
situation, but was derived rather from divine inspiration
and implied distant and mystical promises.

After the destruction of the Jewish state in 70 A.D., the
post-Biblical Jews accepted this concept of prediction as
the most significant aspect of prophetic literature. The
scrupulous analysis of long-past political and military situa-
tions no longer concerned the heirs of the Biblical tradition.
The literary power of the prophets was such that their
works were still read and increasingly searched for mean-
ings relevant to a new age and a new situation. Warnings
of defeat and destruction were no longer meaningful after
the Dispersion, and the temptation to find hidden promises
of restoration and final triumph was overpowering.

Not only did the Jews of the first and second century
A.D. read in the prophets a prediction of the new exile and
a second restoration, but the early Christians found in the
same source predictions of the coming of Jesus and his
messianic role. But just as the dubious quality of prediction
was only retroactively associated with the prophetic writ-

ings, so too was the concept of messianism improperly projected back into the prophetic writings.

It is true that the prophets believed that God would restore His people Israel to their country under the rule of a descendant of the house of David. Anyone who was chosen by the Lord through His prophets to be ruler of His people was regarded as "His messiah," literally, "His anointed." Thus Saul was the "Lord's anointed" (I Samuel 24:7; and frequently), and so were David and Zedekiah (II Samuel 19:22; Lamentations 4:20). Even King Cyrus of Persia, whom the Second Isaiah recognized as God's agent to destroy Babylonia and restore Israel, is described as "His anointed" (Isaiah 45:1). In every case throughout the Biblical period, the "anointed" person was a human being. And when the physical restoration of Israel was contemplated, it was a scion of David who was to be the ruler, the anointed of the Lord. Thus it was Zerubbabel, of the house of David, who led the Restoration of Judah after the Babylonian Exile.

The idea of a superhuman anointed leader, indeed, the very use of the term "Messiah" (with capital "M"), who would be sent down by God at some distant time to intervene directly in behalf of Israel against her oppressors, or in behalf of the righteous against the wicked, is a post-Biblical development in Jewish and Christian circles. Painfully aware that they were unable to cope with the might of Roman imperialism and casting about desperately for comfort and hope in this period of distress and despair, many Jews read back into the Biblical Books the idea and prediction of a superhuman Messiah who would bring deliverance to the Jews at the behest of God. To the Christians, this Messiah was the Christ (from the Greek for "anointed") and Isaiah's young woman with child who would bear a son was the Virgin Mary.

Those who found in the great prophecies the promise of a Messiah tended also to find in the lives of the prophets, with their frequent sufferings, an anticipation of a later, primarily Christian, doctrine of atonement. It became widely assumed that the Second Isaiah, for example, accepted his undeserved suffering meekly and thereby succeeded in sparing his fellow Jews the punishment and doom which was their due for their transgressions against the law and the word of God. According to this doctrine the innocent prophets suffered for the iniquities committed by the people as a whole and served as a substitute for them. There is, however, no basis in the Bible for this principle. It is true that the wickedness of the people was followed by the appearance of the prophets, who as a consequence sometimes suffered abuse; but there is not to be found a single instance in the entire Hebrew Bible where the suffering of a prophet atoned for the sins of a group. Nothing could have been farther from the spirit of the prophetic teachings; that the just and faithful should suffer vicariously, that is, as a substitute, for the unjust and blasphemous, would have been the greatest injustice of all. The prophets insisted on breathing human warmth and understanding into the Law, but they never preached a doctrine which superseded the Covenant and which allowed the sacrifice—in any form—of the innocent in place of the guilty.

By the same canon of justice the prophets frequently found that Israel had suffered sufficient punishment for its sins. Repeated statements to this effect can be found in the Bible; the Second Isaiah himself, for example, far from har-

boring any notions of vicarious atonement, began his series
of unsurpassed compositions to his fellow exiles with this
tender consolation:

> Comfort ye, comfort ye My people,
> says your God,
> Speak tenderly to Jerusalem
> and proclaim unto her
> That her hard service is completed,
> that her punishment is accepted,
> That she has received of the hand of the Lord
> double for all her sins [40: 1–2].

The concept of vicarious suffering and atonement, then,
derives from and has meaning in post-Biblical times when
the Jewish state was destroyed and many Jews exiled from
the land by the Roman conqueror. It was then, in the rab-
binic interpretation, that the "servant of the Lord" in
Isaiah 52:13–53:12—who is none other than the prophet
himself—came to be identified with the people Israel and
Israel came to be regarded as God's servant in suffering
vicariously for the sins of the gentile world. Christianity, by
contrast, identified the "servant of the Lord" with Jesus.
Consequently, the Second Isaiah came to be regarded as
the "suffering" servant of the Lord. In reality, he was no
more a "suffering" servant than Elijah, or Jeremiah, or
Uriah, or Ezekiel. The common term "suffering servant"
is wholly unjustified and misleading in this context.

Particularism and Universality in the Teachings
of the Prophets

Another, perhaps the most important, of the concepts
anachronistically read back into the tradition of the prophets
was the idea that their teachings broadened out until they

encompassed all humanity in a common brotherhood. One of the most frequently quoted, and erroneously interpreted, Bible texts is the well-known passage from Malachi: "Have we not all one father? Has not one God created us?" (2:10). But this verse has been wrenched violently out of its original context when it is made to refer to all mankind. Actually, it charges that the Judean priests of God "have corrupted the Covenant" of the Lord (verses 1–9), that all Israel "has profaned the holiness of the Lord" (verse 11), and that the Lord will punish the transgressors. Malachi's meaning is no different at this point than in the first chapter of his Book, where he proposes that the Lord will destroy Edom if they try to rebuild their land.

The prophetic tradition rests squarely on the idea of the Covenant between the Lord and His people Israel. The prophets were concerned directly and exclusively with this "chosen people," and they took notice of other peoples and nations only when the latter came into contact—invariably for bad rather than good—with Judah and Israel. "Hear this word that the Lord has spoken concerning you," Amos said. "You only, have I recognized of all the families of the earth" (3:1–2). The concept of equality between nations would have been incomprehensible to the prophets or their people. It was an idea which could develop only later and under wholly different circumstances and which, not surprisingly, was read back into the prophetic texts by both Jews and Christians when Rome forced the Jews into exile after A.D. 70 and they found themselves adrift in the vast reaches of the Empire.

The land of Israel which the prophets had known was geographically situated at the military crossroads of the ancient Near East. Its population was small and its possibilities of defense slight, with the result that it knew but few extended periods of peace or freedom from fear of Assyria, Aram, Egypt, and Babylonia. The greatest need and desire of Israel was for peace from her neighbors. Her people were not concerned with the international politics or the welfare of Egypt, Moab, Tyre, or Sidon. Their one concern was to be left alone, and it was this overwhelming desire that Isaiah (2:4) and Micah (4:3) expressed in the famous lines:

> And [the Lord] shall judge between the nations,
>   and He shall decide for many peoples;
> And they shall beat their swords into ploughshares,
>   and their spears into pruning-hooks.
> Nation shall not lift up sword against nation,
>   neither shall they learn war any more.[1]

Read wishfully, this majestic passage might be construed, as it so often has been, to imply a desire for the brotherhood of men and the universal peace on earth. In hard fact, the context excludes this sentimental interpretation. Isaiah and Micah rigidly predicate any such peace on the triumph of Israel. "Out of Zion shall go forth the law," they say, "and the word of the Lord from Jerusalem."

The Second Isaiah, whose moral outlook is generally regarded as the least exclusivist, consistently proclaimed his strongly national point of view. He assures his fellow exiles:

> Thus says the Lord God:
> Behold I will lift up My hand to the nations,
>   and raise My ensign to the peoples;
> And they shall bring your sons in their bosom,

[1] The prophet Joel (4:9 ff.; 3:9 ff. in the English versions), in keeping with the prophetic tradition, put this passage to equally nationalistic use.

and your daughters shall be carried upon their shoulders,
And kings shall be your foster-fathers
   and their queens your nursing mothers.
With their face to the earth they shall bow down to you
   and lick the dust of your feet.
And you shall know that I am the Lord [49:22–23].

In a germinal sense, in the sense that he was elementally responsive to the moods and emotions and sufferings of Israel, the Second Isaiah, as the other prophets, came to express many ideas that took on great meaning for later generations of Jews and Christians alike. Yet within his own historical setting these ideas applied only to his own people. "Awake, awake," he says:

> Put on your strength. O Zion,
> Put on your glorious garments,
>   Jerusalem, Holy City!
> For there shall no more enter you
>   the uncircumsized and the unclean [52:1].

So speaks the prophet that his own people knew and understood, as they had known and understood Amos, Jeremiah, and the rest before him.

At the same time it would be misleading to leave the impression that the prophets' interest stopped short with their own people Israel and went no further. Israel, dwelling among other nations, was intimately and constantly affected by their actions, and the prophets' attention was repeatedly called to include them. The position of their tiny nation in the midst of other, more powerful, nations led the prophets to an outlook that was universal in its ultimate implications. Believing firmly that their God, the only God in existence, would ultimately deliver them from all threats from other nations, so that no more wars would come upon them, consciously aware that the Torah, their religion, was the only code of laws and life by which man could live, the prophets expressed the conviction that all the peoples of the universe, after they had been through stress and strain at the hands of each other through the will of God, would come to realize that Israel and her religion and her God and His abode on Zion—that these constituted the only proper way of life in the entire world. The gentile peoples of the world would then come streaming to the mountain of the Lord's house, to the house of the God of Jacob, in order that, in the words of Isaiah (2:3) and Micah (4:2):

> He may teach us of His ways
>> and we may walk in His paths.
> For out of Zion shall go forth the law,
>> and the word of the Lord from Jerusalem.

While it was the civilization of Israel which the prophets would advocate for the other nations, and while nothing of the gentile cultures was considered worthy of incorporation into the Israelite way of life, the particularism of Israel and her prophetic spokesmen did lay the foundation for the later concept of universality. Gradually it came to be believed that all mankind, by adopting the principles of Israelite belief and practice—that is by accepting the obligations of the Covenant—might enjoy the fruits of God's bounty in the manner that God promised His own people Israel through His prophets. In this universalism, Biblical Israel and her prophets were unique in the Ancient Near East.

When the Jewish descendants of the prophets, during the hellenistic and especially the Roman periods, became more fully aware of living in a single great unified society that encompassed all of the known world, they drew upon and expanded the universalism of the prophets. The prophetic concept of the Covenant had aimed at making all men—of the Israelite society, to be sure—equal in their essential human dignity. This concept, in turn, led to one much broader in scope, of the universality and inevitability of individual moral responsibility toward all men, not merely neighbors and fellow Israelites. It is recorded (Babylonian Talmud, Shabbat 31a) that during the first century B.C. a heathen converted by Hillel, the great exponent of liberalizing Pharisaism in the days of Herod the Great, asked him for a brief exposition of Judaism. Hillel is said to have replied, "What is hateful to you, do not do to your fellow man. This is the whole Law. The rest is mere commentary." Hillel recognized correctly the implication of the Biblical verse: "And you shall love your neighbor as yourself; I am the Lord" (Leviticus 19:18). This precept was incorporated in Christianity and in the western tradition and transmitted from age to age with tremendous impact.

It is to the prophetic tradition more than any other source that western civilization owes its noblest concept of the moral and social obligations of the individual human being. Even if the prophets preached only to their fellow Israelites and saw justice only in the terms of their Covenant with their God, their ringing words have carried from age to age their belief that justice was for the weak as well as for the strong, that its fulfillment was as much a matter of the spirit as the letter of the law, that one could not serve God at the same time that he mistreated his fellow men, that to love God was to love justice, and that the love of justice placed within the conscience of each human being the ultimate inescapable obligation to denounce evil wherever he saw it, to defy a ruler who commanded him to break the Covenant, and to live in the law and the love of God no matter what the cost.

Chronological Summary ～～～～～

ALL dates are approximate and refer to the period B.C.

Before 100,000. *Palaeanthropus palestinensis*, chiefly in the Mount Carmel region of Palestine; a mixed race which stood much closer to Cro-Magnon man (*Homo sapiens*) than to the Neanderthal race.

8000–5500. The Natufian or Mesolithic (Middle Stone) Age in Palestine. Grain was cultivated and prepared, but Natufian man was still far more of a food gatherer (hunting, fishing) than a food producer. Domestication of the dog.

5500–4000. The Neolithic (New, or Late, Stone) Age in Palestine. Villages were established sometimes around shrines. Pottery was introduced. Semites from vast Syrian and Arabian deserts overran the "Fertile Crescent," sometimes to remain. Increased domestication of animals, e.g., sheep. The Near Eastern Neolithic culture preceded the European by several millennia and influenced it considerably.

4000–3300. The Chalcolithic Age. Copper employed as well as flint. Pottery increasingly common.

Writing invented in Mesopotamia. The Jordan and Esdraelon valleys in Palestine settled, as well as other parts of the Near East.

3300–2000.   The Early Bronze Age. Emergence of central states in Mesopotamia and Egypt. Semites and Sumerians in control of Mesopotamia. First empire in history, under Sargon of Akkad.

2000–1500.   The Middle Bronze Age. Emergence of great empires in western Asia and Egypt. Ascendancy of Amorites (western Semites) and Canaanites in western Asia. The patriarchal period. The Mari age. Babylonian empire of Hammurabi (1726–1686), reduced by Hittites (1550). Palestine under Egyptian control. Hyksos invasion and domination of Egypt (1720–1550) and beginning of Hebrew descent into Egypt.

1500–1200.   The Late Bronze Age. Hurrian domination of northern Mesopotamia (the Mitanni Kingdom) (1500–1370), followed by Hittite domination, and then Assyrian (1250). Zenith of Egyptian imperialism ("When Egypt Ruled the East") (1500–1100). Habiru invade and settle in Palestine. Hebrew Exodus from Egypt, under Moses (perhaps shortly after 1300). Wandering in wilderness of Sinai. Conquest of Canaan by Hebrews and Israelites. Term "Israel" first used in triumphal account of campaigns by Merneptah of Egypt (1230).

1200–1000.   The Early Iron Age. Egypt in decline. Assyria the main power in Mesopotamia. Collapse of Canaanite power in Palestine. Invasion of Mediterranean coast of Palestine and Syria by the Philistines and other "sea peoples" from the Aegean regions. Habiru on both sides of the Jordan develop into separate nations: Moabites, Ammonites, Edomites, Israelites. Period of the Judges. Hebrew and Israelite tribes in struggle against the Canaanites and others in their midst and round about them. The Philistine threat spurs on most of the tribes to unite under Saul (1020–1005), Israel's first king.

1005–925. The United Israelite Kingdom under David (1005–965) and Solomon (965–925). The Israelite empire was the dominant power in western Asia.

925–875. The Divided Kingdoms of Israel and Judah. The incursions of Shishak the Egyptian into Israel and Judah resulted in the reduction of Judean prosperity and thus ended her economic and political dominance over Israel. Judah maintained an adequate defence against hostile neighbors and continued to enjoy limited prosperity. Israel was continually faced with a military threat from Aram.

875–750. The Assyrian Threat. The dynasty of Omri, followed by that of Jehu, in Israel continued friendly relations with Phoenicia in response to the continued threat from Aram. The latter part of the ninth century saw the rise of an even greater threat—the warlike Assyrians. Elijah, Elisha, and Amos were prophets in Israel. The judicial and religious reforms of Jehoshaphat in Judah were followed by violent internal struggles over succession to the throne and frequent incursions of Aramean forces. Uzziah (about 780–740) restored internal stability and led Judah to the peak of her power and prosperity.

750–650. The Fall of Israel. The past glories of the Davidic empire were momentarily revived in Israel until Assyrian power overwhelmed her and Israel fell (722). Hosea the prophet in Israel. A narrow margin of prosperity was maintained in Judah under the constant threat of the Assyrian forces. Assyria attacked Judah in force (700) but failed to carry through a definitive conquest. Isaiah and Micah the prophets in Judah.

650–586. The Fall of Judah. The final generation of Judah's independence was marred by frequent conflict with Assyria. Josiah, with the aid of the prophet Jeremiah, put through some religious reforms. Assyrian domination in the Near East was finally broken by Babylonian-Chaldean forces which, under Nebuchadnezzar, conquered Judah (586).

586–539. The Babylonian Captivity. The fall of Jerusalem (586) marked the beginning of the Babylonian Exile which was ended in 539 by the Edict of Liberation of Cyrus the Persian, conqueror of Babylon-Chaldea. Ezekiel and Second Isaiah the prophets of the Exile.

539–400. The First Return to Judah. Zerubbabel and

Joshua the secular and religious heads of Judea. Haggai and Zechariah the prophets in Judea. Temple in Jerusalem rebuilt.

400. The Second Return, and Hellenistic civilization. Second return to Judah, under Ezra. Jewish colonies in Egypt. Jewish theocracy established in Judea by Ezra and Nehemiah. The high priests rule Judea.

300. Hellenistic civilization overwhelms Western Asia and Egypt, following the conquests by Alexander the Great.

Suggestions for Further Reading

IN understanding the development of western civilization the Bible is unquestionably the most important single text, and no heir to this tradition who has not read it can consider himself educated. Of the translations available in English the best are *The Revised Standard Version of the Old Testament* (New York, 1952) and *The Old Testament—an American Translation*, rev. ed. by T. J. Meek (Chicago; several printings). A new translation (editor-in-chief H. M. Orlinsky) is now in progress of *The Holy Scriptures according to the Masoretic Text*, editor-in-chief M. L. Margolis (Jewish Publication Society, Philadelphia, 1917); *The Torah: The Five Books of Moses* appeared in 1962.

For those who would consult introductions along critical lines there are G. W. Anderson, *A Critical Introduction to the Old Testament* (London, 1959); S. R. Driver, *An Introduction to the Literature of the Old Testament* (New York, 1914; now a Meridian paperback); R. H. Pfeiffer, *The Books of the Old Testament* (New York, 1957; an abridgment of his detailed *Introduction to the Old Testament*, 1941). A conservative approach is followed in S. B. Freehof's *Preface to Scripture* (Cincinnati, 1950).

Only in more recent times has the Hebrew Bible been treated as literature. Richard G. Moulton, *The Literary Study of the Bible*, rev. ed. (Boston, 1899), and the companion volume, *The Modern Reader's Bible* (New York, 1930), are worth reading. The Biblical literature is treated in broad perspective by H. M. and N. K. Chadwick, *The Growth of Literature* (2 vols.; Cambridge, Eng., 1936), in Vol. II, pp. 629–777.

The history of the Biblical period is subject to more frequent and serious change than that of any other, both because of the constant discovery of new texts and materials and the consequent reinterpretation of the older data. Whoever wishes to keep up with the latest discoveries and trends in the history of ancient Israel would do well to read regularly *The Biblical Archaeologist* (American Schools of Oriental Research, New Haven; subscription $2.00 per year, for four issues). Ralph E. Turner's *The Great Cultural Traditions, the Foundations of Civilization* (2 vols.; New York and London, 1941), serves as a useful introduction to the ancient world in general, though the specific sections on ancient Israel (pp. 329–359, 697–734) need revision. Useful books on the beginnings of history are V. Gordon Childe's *Man Makes Himself* (Mentor Book, 1951), *New Light on the Most Ancient East*, 4th ed. (London, 1952), and *What Happened in History* (Pelican Book, 1954). A serviceable popular survey of the ancient Near East is S. Moscati, *The Face of the Ancient Orient* (London, 1960). H. Frankfort's *The Birth of Civilization in the Near East* (Anchor Book, 1950) is a penetrating study. *Ancient Near Eastern Texts Relating to the Old Testament*, 2d ed., ed. J. B. Pritchard (Princeton, 1955), and the companion volume, *The Ancient Near East in Pictures* (1954), constitute an excellent collection of documents which shed direct and indirect light on the Hebrew Bible; *The Ancient Near East: an Anthology of Texts and Pictures* (1958) is a compendium of the two. I. Mendelsohn edited *Religions of the Ancient Near East: Sumero-Akkadian Religious Texts and Ugaritic Epics* (New York, 1955). A useful work is *Documents from Old Testament Times*, ed. D. Winton Thomas (New York, 1958). *The Intellectual Adventure of Ancient Man*, ed. H. and H. A. Frankfort (Chicago, 1946), with chapters on Egypt (by J. A. Wilson), Mesopotamia (by T. Jacobsen), and the Hebrews (by W. A. Irwin), is an integrated attempt to explain the thinking of the ancient Near East; this volume (without the chapters on the Hebrews) appeared as *Before Philosophy* (Pelican Books, 1949). *The Idea of History in the Ancient Near East,* ed. R. C. Dentan (New Haven, 1955); *Authority and Law in the Ancient Orient* (1954; monograph supplement to *Journal of the American Oriental Society*); S. N. Kramer, *History Begins at Sumer* (Anchor Book, 1959); J. A. Wilson, *The Burden of Egypt* (Chicago, 1951; now a Phoenix paperback); G. Steindorff and K. C. Seele, *When Egypt Ruled the East,* rev. ed. (Chicago, 1957); C. H. Gordon, *The World of the Old Testament* (Garden City, N.Y., 1958); the "General Articles" in Vol. I (pp. 3–46) of *The Interpreter's Bible* (New York and Nashville, 1952)—all these have much to offer the student of ancient Israel.

The historical geography of Palestine has been very well treated by G. E. Wright and F. V. Filson in *The Westminster Historical Atlas to the Bible,* 2d ed. (Philadelphia, 1956); the text of this book constitutes also a fine sketch of Biblical Israel's history. The same may be said of N. Glueck, *The River Jordan, being an Illustrated Account of Earth's Most Storied River* (Philadelphia, 1946). Other recent works of note in this area are L. H. Grollengberg's *Atlas of the Bible* (New York, 1956); E. G. Kraeling's *Bible Atlas* (Chicago, 1956); Denis Baly, *The Geography of the Bible* (New York, 1957).

In the category of Biblical archaeology there are a number of good works, e.g., J. Finegan, *Light from the Ancient Past,* rev. ed. (Princeton, 1959); G. E. Wright, *Biblical Archaeology* (Philadelphia, 1957); W. F. Albright, *The Archaeology of Palestine* (Pelican Book, 1949); A. Parrot, *Discovering Buried Worlds* and *Studies in Biblical Archaeology,* nos. 1–8 (New York, 1955—); J. B. Pritchard, *Archaeology and the Old Testament* (Princeton, 1958).

There are now available two fine works on Israel's career:

M. Noth, *The History of Israel* (New York, 1958); and J. Bright, *A History of Israel* (Philadelphia, 1959). A well-ordered and stimulating attempt to reconstruct the origin and development of Israel, her Law, her concept of God, her priesthood, and her prophets, may be found in T. J. Meek's *Hebrew Origins*, rev. ed. (New York, 1950; Torch Books, 1959). F. James's *Personalities of the Old Testament* (New York, 1945) is the best of its kind. There is nothing quite like *Views of the Biblical World* (in natural-color photography), ed. B. Mazar, M. Avi-Yonah, A. Malamat, *et. al.*, Vol. I: *The Law* (Jerusalem, 1958), following the chapter-and-verse order of the Bible; in Volumes II–V it is planned to cover the New Testament as well as the Old.

A comprehensive survey of "Old Testament Studies" in the United States and Canada during the period 1930–1962 constitutes Chapter II, by H. M. Orlinsky, in *Religion*, ed. P. Ramsey (Englewood Cliffs, N. J., 1965; Vol. XIII in The Princeton Studies: Humanistic Scholarship in America), pp. 51–109.

Index

Place names have been localized on at least one of the five maps; thus Jerusalem (II B 4-5) indicates that Jerusalem may be identified on Map II at B longitudinally and 4-5 latitudinally.